Garbo

Garbo

NORMAN ZIEROLD

STEIN AND DAY/*Publishers*/New York

for
Marguerite Young
and
Robert Halsband

Copyright © 1969 by Norman Zierold
Library of Congress Catalog Card No. 69-17936
All rights reserved

Published simultaneously in Canada by Saunders of Toronto, Ltd.
Designed by Bernard Schleifer
Manufactured in the United States of America
Stein and Day/*Publishers*/7 East 48 Street, New York, N.Y. 10017

SBN 8128-1212-3

Contents

Acknowledgments

INTEREST IN Greta Garbo has been so intense over the years that a number of people who know or knew her have been repeatedly besieged by requests for interviews. I am grateful to those who were willing to search their memories once more for insight and details, and give me their changing perspective of a legendary woman. I am doubly indebted to those never interviewed before, who gave of their time knowing that they were risking the loss of Garbo's friendship by speaking of her.

A word of thanks, too, to the biographers who went before —notably, John Bainbridge's evocative, thoughtful *Garbo*, now out of print; Fritiof Billquist's *Garbo*, the best source available on the early years, given a lesser emphasis here because of that book's thoroughness and excellence; and *Greta Garbo*, by Raymond Durgnat and John Kobal. Earlier short works by Ruth Biery, Ake Sundborg, and Rilla Page Palmborg proved valuable, as did the magazine and newspaper reportage relating to Garbo, a voluminous mass extending to the present day.

Garbo and
Her Mystique

THE ANCIENT GREEKS had their mythological gods and goddesses; the medieval period its saints; and later came kings and queens. For the modern age, especially during Hollywood's gaudiest days, the equivalent objects of worship and adoration were the stars of the motion picture screen. These were manufactured for a ravenous public by giant studios like Metro-Goldwyn-Mayer, Paramount, and Warner Brothers, each headed by tenacious, dedicated tyrants whose origins reached back to the ghettos of Europe. Under their aegis elaborate publicity buildups, column upon column of print supplemented by imaginative photography, were used to forge film personalities. When the public responded, it was said that a star was born.

The public and private images of stars often blended easily. Douglas Fairbanks on screen portrayed swash-buckling heroes; in private life he was a romantic, flamboyant daredevil. The real Humphrey Bogart was less tough and crusty than his screen counterpart, but the

two personalities were basically harmonious. Gary
Cooper was strong and silent both on-screen and off.
Katherine Hepburn often portrayed brittle, bright
women with an underlying warmth and sensitivity,
women much like herself.

At the other end of the spectrum, the performer's
public image could be at great variance with the true
self. Theda Bara, the screen's first man-destroying vamp,
was a nice Jewish girl from Cincinnati who never
vamped anyone offscreen. After fighting unsuccessfully
for contrasting roles, she retired early from the movies
to become a contented housewife. Rudolph Valentino, a
simple Italian boy who tried to live up to his screen
image as the great masculine lover, destroyed himself in
the process. The conflicts and tensions of stardom have
exacted a heavy toll over the years, one brought into
perspective by the very mention of such figures of
tragedy as Wallace Reid, Mabel Normand, John Gilbert,
Valentino, Jean Harlow, and Marilyn Monroe.

For the subject of this book, a woman whose legend
has already outlived her screen apogee by nearly three
decades, life has been neither tragic nor placid. The
tensions inherent in her situation could not be brushed
aside, but neither did they lead her to drugs, or alcohol,
or suicide. Her creative nature, at once instinctive,
shrewd, and forceful, enabled her to walk the high wire
of her extraordinary fame and to reconcile that fame
with her inner needs.

The product of a Swedish peasant household, Greta
Garbo came to Hollywood in 1925, during the period
of the great studios. The movies, still silent, were already international in scope and influence. Charlie Chap-

lin was the *world's* favorite comedian. Mary Pickford was "America's Sweetheart," but her popularity extended far beyond America. Gloria Swanson, the screen incarnation of the sophisticated woman, improved upon the role by going to France and marrying a bonafide marquis.

Garbo was something new for Hollywood. She was tall and broad-shouldered at a time when female stars were usually petite; pensive and reserved where the order of the day was flamboyance. The studio was in a quandary as to how to market her when suddenly the direction became clear. She was cast in her first film, *The Torrent,* and the response was electrifying.

Audiences responded to a series of patterns which she was able to project. As a love object she combined the sensual with a spiritual appeal, femininity with a mannish quotient; she was as attractive to women as to men. At the same time she seemed emotionally and philosophically wary, detached, passive. Her face, early called the face of the century, had an extraordinary plasticity, a mirror-like quality; people could see in it their own conflicts and desires.

This unique combination proved magnetic to a nation presumably in the heedless throes of the Era of Good Feeling. Garbo reflected the malaise, the nervous discontent underlying the surface. Through a combination of art, artifice, and accident, she began to capture the public imagination as a romantic, suffering recluse— a world-weary woman who went through the motions of living but who seemed always to foresee despair ahead.

Once this mystique began to germinate, it fed on

itself, abetted by directors and co-stars, by promotion executives and the press—and by the public, for whom the real Garbo became one with the myth. In reality, the two were not identical. The public image obscured the private person, and Garbo herself remained basically unknown. Even her numerous biographers failed to see that the mystique expressed only one side of Garbo, that it was always sparked by an active, volatile personality. Stars do not reach the heights through passivity.

The fact is that Garbo, world symbol of the charismatic loner, has virtually done everything, gone everywhere, seen everyone. She has managed to live her own richly peopled life while simultaneously retaining her mystique, assuring its survival long after her departure from films. The feat constitutes one of the bravura performances of our time.

How did she do it? Largely by protesting all the way to the studio. She saw many people and said she valued, above all, her privacy. She loved and said it was only friendship. She made films that aroused worldwide admiration and said it was all a pain, that Hollywood was alien to art, that it was her "cloister." She sailed around the world on spacious yachts, surrounded by international celebrities, and said it was a bore.

In these pages she is quoted on a wide range of subjects, from love and children to privacy and God. But in telling the world she has nothing to say, and that in any event it is all no one's business but her own, she has given the impression that she is unquotable and silent. Her entire life is her greatest role.

A case in point is her 1928 *The Story of Greta Garbo*—as told by her to Ruth Biery. It begins:

"Let's not talk of me. It is New Year's Eve. In Sweden that means so much, so very much. There we go to church and eat and drink and see everyone we know. I have been sad all day—at home in Sweden they are skiing and skating and throwing snowballs at one another. Their cheeks are red—oh, please let's not talk of me."

And on goes Greta to not talk about her family:

"I don't want the world to talk about my mother and father. Nor my brother, nor my sister. . . . Why should I tell the world about them? They are mine!"

And her attitudes:

"There are many things in your heart you can never tell to another person. They are you, your private joys and sorrows, and you can never tell them. You cheapen yourself, the inside of yourself when you tell them."

After these rather tame quotations appeared in print, Garbo told Ruth Biery: "I do not like your story. I do not like to see my soul laid bare upon paper."

In her other early biography, *That Gustafsson Girl* by Ake Sundborg, she took precisely the same tack:

"The story of my life? We all do the same things. We go to school, we learn, we grow up—one much as another. What does it matter who my parents were, or what they did. I cannot see what significance these facts have for others. We gradually find our aim in life and try to fulfill its' mission. This is the significance of life. The result of our life should bear witness to what we are, what we will do, what we can achieve. And our work tells this best in its own language. Mine happens to be the language of the motion picture screen."

Greta Garbo has always insisted she has nothing to

say—while saying quite pertinent things. This ingenious, no doubt at first unconscious device has been a key ingredient of her star quality; she has let us know aspects of herself and yet always reserved certain areas of experience, thereby implicitly assigning a very high value to her personality.

Garbo in the flesh, it becomes increasingly clear, was never as mysterious as the mystique would have it, nor as aloof and distant, nor as weary and detached, nor as simple. Over the years she did indeed suffer from the constant exposure to public scrutiny, but she developed defenses and ploys which enabled her to express many facets of her highly original nature. Eventually she came to accept the role she was called upon to play, to see it in a perspective that allowed her to enjoy it, and even to strive consciously to perpetuate it.

With the passing of the old-time studios, star worship has drastically declined. One has only to compare the popularity of a latter-day figure like Ann-Margaret, shifting from company to company, to stars nurtured by MGM's factory—Elizabeth Taylor, Spencer Tracy, Judy Garland. But then, even in Hollywood's most glamorous days, there was only one Garbo.

The adoration Garbo aroused bordered on frenzy; those most seriously afflicted were termed Garbomaniacs. She also inspired skepticism, fierce antagonisms, and the kind of misunderstandings and misconceptions which continue to this day. Strong-willed and resilient, Garbo survived a harrowing series of critical onslaughts at the very height of her fame, as the comments which follow reveal. Their range and intensity are a measure of the extent to which she had become, in the thirties, a national obsession:

". . . Garbo will be forgotten as a woman in ten years, and as an actress her memory will be dead when Helen Hayes's, Lynn Fontanne's, and Katherine Cornell's are beginning to grow greenest."

So wrote Clare Boothe Luce, then Clare Boothe Brokaw, in "The Great Garbo," an article which ran in the February 1932 issue of *Vanity Fair*. In her clouded crystal ball she saw that history "had never reserved a place for a beautiful woman who did not love, or who was not loved by, at least one interesting, powerful, or brilliant man"—Helen brought to mind Menelaus and Paris; Cleopatra, Caesar and Mark Antony. For Garbo there was only John Gilbert, and her romance with that actor was "a standard product of the Hollywood flesh-pots."

Unless she remedied the "oversight" of not having had a great love, Clare continued, "those shadowy, gigantic six-foot closeup embraces, the microphoned passions spent in the arms of celluloid Gilberts, Novarros, Montgomerys, and Gables will be her only epitaph —faintly humorous celluloid strips of interest only to antiquarians or other-day humorists who may conceivably show them to their friends to provide a curious or mirthful evening."

After spending many lines backtracking, explaining that "her magnetism and her allure . . . far transcend her beauty, as they also transcend her ability as an actress," Clare concluded her piece with these words:

"Selfish, shrewd, ignorant, self-absorbed and whimsical, perverse and innocent—she is the perfect realization of the child left to itself, unhampered and uncontrolled by mature authority. Every man has the love affairs he deserves. . . . Our generation's loveliest woman is but a phantom upon a silver screen—a shadow with the face of an angel of perdition, as substantial as a mist before the moon, the inarticulate, the bad-tempered, and the 'great' Garbo."

A 1931 *New Yorker* profile by Virgilia Peterson Ross began dramatically: "Six lively people were gathered in someone's Hollywood drawing room one rainy night when the doorbell rang and Miss Greta Garbo was announced. She came in wearing a beret over her straight blonde hair, a tailored suit, a man's shirt and tie, and a pair of flat-heeled shoes. When the guests saw her face, their talk abruptly died away. She sat silent while they made sporadic comments on the weather and stole furtive looks at her. She was alone, bottled in by a childish lack of interest, inarticulate, uncomfortable, offering no access to herself. She was unwilling, perhaps unable, to share in the social responsibilities of the occasion. She had made the effort to come, and now, awkwardly, she hid behind her beauty. The party soon scattered. Garbo had frozen the evening."

Seldom has a writer evoked more hostility than Katherine Albert, a one-time MGM publicist who let fly at the Garbo mystique in a 1930 issue of *Photoplay*. "What goes on within her mind as she paces up and down the set, back and forth, you nor I will ever know," she wrote sacrilegiously. "Mystery? She may be thinking the most profound of thoughts. She may be wondering if her herring will be chopped properly for dinner. . . ."

The piece was only a prelude to "Exploding the Garbo Myth," which appeared in April of the following year: "Dust off the old family shotgun, prepare the burning oil, do with me as you will," it began. "I've simply got to say it. I'm bored with Garbo!"

Miss Albert obviously was aware that one cannot attack goddesses with impunity. Curiously—considering the violent reaction it provoked—the article said many flattering things about Garbo, describing her as having a unique hold on the imagination of the people, as occupying in fact the highest place in all the film firmament. Garbomaniacs brushed aside the complimentary remarks, infuriated as they read that directors and studio executives had confided Garbo was "no great shakes as an actress," that what had been called great artistry was "no more or less than a facial trick which in some way piques the imagination."

"Rudolph Valentino had a dead nerve in one eyelid," Miss Albert explained. "It gave that eyelid a droop. And a nice, wholesome Italian boy became the sinister, mysterious dream-lover of a million women. Garbo appeals in the same way."

No sooner was the magazine on the newsstands than letters of condemnation began flooding in to *Photoplay* publisher James Quirk—a startling fifteen thousand in all, many of them threatening cancellation of subscriptions. "The reaction to a critical article written by Katherine Albert, who dared to question the artistic dimensions and divinity of Garbo, was the most amazing in the history of this publication," Quirk stated in an editorial. He ordered all bulky packages addressed to Miss Albert delivered to the Police Bomb Squad.

Hobo reporter Jim Tully, one of the era's favorite columnists, put his popularity on the line with a stinging diatribe. "The Swedish film actress is phlegmatic, even apathetic," he wrote. "Of the fire that sets the white screen ablaze only the ash is visible in ordinary life. She is broad-shouldered, flat-chested, awkward in her movements. Her figure is the seamstress' despair. She has no real beauty, but with clever lighting and photographing, she becomes graceful and fascinating on the screen. . . . Garbo is the only woman in the world who has made capital out of her anemia. Her indolent movements and half-shut eyes give an impression of exotic sensuality. The real reason for them is fatigue. She is just no longer able to keep her mouth shut or her eyes open. . . ."

The most belligerent of the anti-Garbo faction was Don Herold of *The Commonwealth*. *Camille*, considered by many to be Garbo's masterpiece, provoked a broadside from Herold at the time:

"I object fundamentally to the Garbo type of film in the first place. Love is invariably magnified to pathological importance—I have previously said that Garbo is sex on a high horse. I dislike the possible effects on the rising generation of the philosophy of love in the usual Garbo film. I prefer even the more wholesome, more profane Mae West philosophy: if it works, fine; if not, 'Beulah, peel me a grape.'

"Detach yourself from the Garbo spell at any point in almost any Garbo picture, slap yourself back to common sense, listen to her as you might to any woman, and you'll realize what horsefeathers most of the Garbo technique is. There is too much glum severity or knowing laughter (with head thrown back). It is all too thick, all too, too significant. I say 'it's spinach.' "

Even the celebrated Garbo voice failed to impress one English critic who described it as "ugly, throaty, raw, and full of German gutturals."

Finally, there was Herbert Kretzmer's lament at the end of a long article: "Garbo: why can't she leave us alone? She has flogged her childish game of peek-a-boo to death. Boiled down to essentials, she is a plain mortal girl with large feet."

Garbo has eluded those who showered her with abuse and those who worshipped. Both have mistakenly seen her in terms of absolutes when in reality hers has always been, to an extraordinary degree, an adaptive, evolving personality. She has confounded the skeptics, the scoffers, and the pundits gazing into their clouded crystals. Even after long retirement her mystique continues to thrive, surely one of the most enduring obsessions of the twentieth century.

She made her last film in 1941 as World War II was reaching a crescendo. During the desperate hours of the Battle of Britain, Winston Churchill sought relaxation in a projection room where Garbo films flickered across the screen. On the Axis side, Adolf Hitler asked for them—even when their directors were of proscribed Jewish origin.

After the war, Metro-Goldwyn-Mayer underwent a series of crises as television and foreign films invaded the market. Garbo's old mentor, Louis B. Mayer, was thrust from power. Her films, relegated to the warehouse, were almost never seen in the late forties or in the fifties.

The public, no longer exposed to her films, remained fascinated by the star herself. As she pursued her quest for privacy, she was forced to flee from photographers lying in wait at airports, on shipboard, on the streets of world capitals. *Look,* and *Life,* and *Paris-Match,* and *Oggi,* even *Women's Wear Daily* flaunted the prying camera's every glimpse of the retired star.

In the early sixties, a distributor in Southern California began readying a Garbo Film Festival. Predictably it awakened surviving members of an elderly tribe, the Garbo nay-sayers. One was Phil Scheuer of the Los Angeles *Times:* "I am not at all sure the spell has renewed itself for a later generation. Today, auras of mystery are no longer popular; impatiently we rip them away." The Los Angeles *Herald Examiner* critic agreed: "I question the festival's prospects for success. I'll wager most of the patrons will be older, will be going to recapture part of their past as much as anything else."

Variety's headline when the festival opened was simple: "BOFFO BIZ." Huge turnouts startled the new regime at MGM, and prints of the Garbo pictures were hastily made. Another festival, in England, drew sell-out audiences. Italy's one television network scheduled five Sunday evenings of Garbo films; they attracted viewers in record numbers and led to a new Garbo fad in fashion. "She's the hottest thing we've had since Perry Mason," said a network official.

In 1968 the Museum of Modern Art in New York announced a festival which would show all the Garbo films except *The Divine Woman,* of which no print could be found. Old and young people bought out every available ticket far in advance. The entire repertory, the early European films as well as the American, eventually was scheduled for a rerun.

As the incantatory spell of Garbo renewed itself for the sixties, speculation about the actress, the woman, and the mystique began anew. The producer of an American television documentary on Garbo made an interesting observation:

"If you look at the Swedish pictures, her early comic films, you see she's a WAMPAS baby star, the Mary Carlisle of Sweden. The films are absolutely idiotic, and there is no mystery to Garbo—the early pictures bear no relation to the woman who comes later. Somebody invented this woman, recognizing that there was an extraordinary inner core."

Garbo's plasticity made it possible for her to reflect the fantasies of her screen audience; in this sense she functioned as a receptacle for the emotions of others. In real life she indeed operated from "an extraordinary inner core," but here too she displayed a certain passivity, was open, ready to absorb and assimilate, especially from strong, volatile personalities. At the very beginning of her career she came under the influence of Sweden's foremost director, Mauritz Stiller. If anyone "invented" Garbo, it was he.

Stiller
and Garbo

THE FATEFUL ENCOUNTER that brought Greta Gustafsson into Stiller's life took place in the spring of 1923.
He was then forty, the guiding genius of Sweden's
highly acclaimed cinema; she was seventeen, a drama
student on a scholarship at the Royal Dramatic Theatre
in Stockholm. Poverty and severe strain had marked
the background of both.

Both Greta's mother, plump and florid, and her fine-
boned and sensitive father were of peasant background.
Lacking education, the father worked as an unskilled
laborer in Stockholm. He was often ill or unemployed.
One of the lasting impressions of Greta's childhood was
her visits with him to a charity clinic.

The family, including an older brother and sister,
Sven and Alva, lived in a coldwater flat, four rooms of
a fourth-floor walkup, at 32 Blekingegaten Street. The
neighborhood was drab, but there were theatres nearby.
Greta began very early to linger at the stage doors, was
not yet in her teens when she developed a schoolgirl

25

crush on Carl Brisson, the handsome Danish boxer turned actor. At the homes of friends she liked to perform in improvised skits.

Fully grown at twelve, Greta was self-conscious about her appearance. "My size embarrassed me horribly," she told one of her first biographers. "Everywhere people seemed to be whispering about my awkwardness.

"There isn't much to tell of my school years," she went on. "I went to public school and hated it. I hated its confinement, its repression. Unlike most children, I dreaded recess. I could not bear the thought of playing by order, by the clock, in the schoolyard. . . .

"Though I am the youngest of three children, my brother and sister always looked on me as the oldest. In fact I can hardly remember ever having felt young in the ordinary sense. I always had opinions, and the others looked to me for decisions and for the solutions to their problems. . . .

"Even when I was a tiny girl, I preferred being alone. . . . I could give my imagination free rein and live in a world of lovely dreams. . . . My moods were changeable. Happy one moment—the next plunged in despair."

Greta's father died when she was fourteen. Alva went to work as a stenographer, Greta as a lather girl in a neighborhood barbershop. From there she graduated to Paul U. Bergstrom's Department Store, usually referred to as PUB. As a salesgirl in the millinery section she was paid 125 kronor a month, about twenty-five dollars.

When Captain Ragnar Ring, the head of a firm

which produced advertising films, came to PUB to make a short subject called *How Not to Dress*, Greta's experience in modeling hats led to a small comic role. Ring later put her into another promotional film for bakery products, *Our Daily Bread*. Again her role was comic— in one scene she gorged herself on a cream puff, in another she devoured cookies at an island picnic.

The brief experiences before the camera delighted Greta. On learning that a visitor to PUB, director Erik Petschler, was casting a feature film, she approached him boldly. He asked her to recite something for him, a school poem as it turned out, and cast her in *Peter the Tramp*. Since Petschler was a Scandinavian Mack Sennett, Greta's first movie appearance was in a comedy.

"Since Miss Gustafsson has so far had only the dubious pleasure of having to play a 'Bathing Beauty' for Mr. Erik A. Petschler in his fire department film, we have received no impression whatever of her capacity," wrote the critic of the Swedish magazine *Swing* in 1923. "It pleases us, though, to have the opportunity of noting a new name in Swedish films and we hope to have a chance to mention it again." A photo accompanying the article carried an interesting caption: "Greta Gustafsson. May perhaps become a Swedish film star. Reason: her Anglo-Saxon appearance."

Slight praise was sufficient. Greta decided to pursue her new career. On her card at PUB she wrote her reason for leaving: "To enter the films." On the advice of Petschler she sought the professional training which eventually led her to the Royal Academy.

She entered that distinguished training ground for Sweden's finest actors on a scholarship. A serious student, she played several small roles at the Royal Dramatic Theatre. At the time she met Stiller, there were no signs as yet of an unusual gift.

Stiller's early background formed a colorful but troubled prelude to success. His father, a Ruthenian Jew serving in the musician's corps of the Russian Army, married the daughter of a Jewish doctor from Poland. In Helsinki the Stillers raised a family of six children, Mauritz being the fourth. When he was three, both parents died within a matter of months, the father through illness, the mother by suicide.

The Stiller children were boarded out to various families, Mauritz with a hat manufacturer named Katzmann. At grammar school his record as a student was erratic, but his rambunctious practical jokes and his gift for mimicry made him a favorite with the other pupils. In his teens he went to work as a salesman for his foster father. His efforts were unsatisfactory, and his interest gradually shifted to the theatre, where he acted in various local groups.

In 1904, civil disorders in Helsinki led to a call-up of all males over twenty-one. Stiller submitted to a medical examination, the results of which he mistakenly interpreted as a failure to meet required standards. He neglected to report for duty, was arrested and sentenced to six years of military service, half to be spent in Siberia. Temperamental and headstrong, he deserted, using a false passport to make his way to Sweden, whose language he spoke.

The next years brought a trying succession of part-time jobs and bit parts in obscure provincial theatres. As a performer, Stiller left much to be desired. He was egotistical, chafed at discipline, overacted. In 1911 Sweden's first film studio, Biograph, opened its doors. Stiller, taken on as an actor, disliked what he saw. He used his very considerable powers of persuasion to talk the studio into letting him direct. Here his unique gifts—extreme sensitivity linked to an eccentric but authoritative personality—led to immediate advancement.

In the next decade he made forty films, many of them two-reel thrillers. His reputation rested, however, on two important features. *Sir Arne's Treasure*, in 1919, was a tale of crime and punishment which made a forward-looking attempt to delineate human character. In 1920 came *Erotikon*, a sophisticated look at marriage. Critics called it the first modern comedy, a large leap ahead from the slapstick farces of the Mack Sennett school.

In his major efforts Stiller was an authentic innovator, not unlike D. W. Griffith. He was the first European director to use closeups, to employ the shifting camera, to develop new and striking camera angles. He was exuberant and also painstaking. His highly developed sense of beauty and drama gave his films an easily recognizable style.

"I venture the paradox that films, as well as stage productions, ought to be played by amateurs, if they could only do it," he said on one occasion. "When an actor is truly great he is always trying to get back to the natural simplicity that was his when he knew nothing about the techniques of acting."

Stiller often went into the streets to find his performers—and into the Royal Academy, where he sought apprentice players whose acting technique had not yet solidified into a fixed style.

The film he was planning in 1923 was to be an adaptation of *The Saga of Gösta Berling*, by Nobel Prize-winner Selma Lagerlof. The novel recounts the adventures of a hard-living hero, a pastor with a penchant for worldly pleasures. Dismissed from the pulpit, Gösta becomes tutor to the daughter of the Mistress of Ekeby. The daughter's sister-in-law, Italian Countess Elizabeth Dohna, falls in love with him, and her purity of heart helps to redeem him. Not, however, before a series of melodramatic episodes, including a spectacular fire and a ride across the ice with howling wolves in pursuit.

Already cast in the title role was Lars Hanson, the popular leading man of the Swedish cinema. Veteran actress Gerda Lundequist was to play the female lead, the Mistress of Ekeby. To Gustav Molander, director of the Academy, Stiller said he was still seeking to fill two roles—that of the Countess Ebba Dohna and the Countess Elizabeth Dohna, the latter the second female lead. For these he wanted talented but as yet unknown and unformed actresses. Molander recommended Mona Martenson and Greta Gustafsson. Mona, a second-year student, was known to Stiller, who cast her as Countess Ebba Dohna. Greta was given an appointment to see Stiller at his home.

She was understandably apprehensive. Stiller's magnetic and flamboyant personality had imposed itself firmly on Stockholm, complementing his professional reputation. Hardly handsome, he was nonetheless striking in appearance, a sturdily built six-footer with large feet and great outsized hands. His long face was dominated by intense gray eyes with heavy brows, a strong nose, a bristling moustache. His wavy hair was short-cropped and silver-gray.

Stiller's manner could only be described as dashing, with London tailors supplying their most fashionable cuts. Fur coats reaching almost to the snow-covered ground were a Stiller touch, as were richly patterned ties and a dazzling display of jewelry—rings, tie pins, diamond studs.

Around Stockholm Stiller's Kissel Kar, a custom-made canary-yellow roadster, was a familiar sight. It became known as the Yellow Peril: Stiller often floored the accelerator only to find himself bolting backward, having mistakenly put the gearshift into reverse.

From press accounts, impressionable young actresses like Greta Gustafsson learned that the good life was very much to Stiller's taste, that he demanded and got the best in food and drink, luxurious apartments or hotel accommodations. With friends he was alternately capable of grand gestures of generosity and of petty borrowings; cigarettes or small sums seldom repaid. He was known to be moody, elated one moment and then, in the manner of the true northerner, suddenly depressed. He could exude arrogant self-confidence and then withdraw into self-deprecation and recriminations; he would bellow at co-workers when under pressure and then make amends with a touching warmth and attractiveness.

His mind was lightning quick. In conversation, his remarks sometimes seemed puzzling because logical bridges had been omitted; a series of non-sequiturs would be followed by questions only half posed before he himself answered them.

On the day of his meeting with Greta Gustafsson, she arrived nervous and fearful. Mauritz Stiller entered belatedly with Charlie, his huge French bulldog. Without speaking he looked intently at the young Academy student. After a time he made small talk, observing her carefully while seeming to be occupied with small errands in the room.

"Let me have your telephone number," he finally said, and dismissed her.

She returned home discouraged, not expecting to hear further. A candid look into the mirror did not lift her spirits. The simple dress, the dark low-heeled shoes, the black stockings were perhaps all too understated. She was too heavy, her hair was frizzy, her teeth uneven.

Mauritz Stiller had seen all that—and much more. "I immediately noticed how easily one could dominate her by looking straight into her eyes," he wrote in his diary.

Several days later he placed a call which brought her to Rasunda Film City to test for the role of Elizabeth Dohna. Greta, again frightened and ill at ease, took a streetcar to the studio.

When she arrived Stiller issued his first directive: "You must lose at least twenty pounds if you're to get this part."

Associates of the director looked at the awkward girl and were unimpressed. They knew that Stiller had long dreamed of molding an extraordinary woman, exalted and worldly but with an underlying feminine grace—as he himself put it, "supersensual, spiritual, and mystic."

"Be sick," he told his unlikely candidate, pointing to a bed. Greta lay down and attempted to look wan. Stiller was furious, demanding to know if she had never been really ill. She tried again and the results were better.

"She is green, and has no technique, and cannot show her feelings now," Stiller confided to a friend. "But she will be right. I'll see to that. And her face! You only get a face like that in front of a camera once in a century."

It was late July when Greta signed a contract to play the Countess Elizabeth Dohna. Her salary came to six hundred dollars for what was to be half a year's work. Stiller, his head high in nimbus clouds when it came to art, invariably drove a hard bargain in money matters.

The Saga of Gösta Berling was an ambitious, expensive project, with important stars and elaborate multiple sets. What drew everyone's attention, however, was the relationship which developed between the difficult, demanding director and his young protégée. Greta at this time was young, healthy, sunny-tempered. She knew she was being given a great opportunity and was fiercely determined to fulfill her mentor's expectations. As a result she was extremely tense, so nervous that on the first day of shooting she was unable to work at all. Thereafter she developed a facial tic which made it difficult to photograph her in closeup.

Stiller, a restless, ruthless perfectionist, did not make things easier. Every aspect of her performance came under his scrutiny, her hair, her makeup, the lighting. Inexhaustibly patient during long hours of rehearsal, he would suddenly burst into a rage when a movement was less graceful than he wanted. He would shout, bluster, wheedle, plead, cajole. Greta would try again and again, finally dissolving into tears. When she did, Stiller was invariably gentle. He would place his great hand on her shoulder; draw her close and remind her that he was doing it all for her.

He also talked, endlessly, explaining what the role called for, what it meant in terms of dedication to be an actress. During breaks in the shooting, other cast members would see the master walking with his pupil in a small grove outside the studio. Stiller would be speaking, Greta bending her head attentively, listening. The strange pair was nicknamed Beauty and the Beast.

Greta soon was seen at Stiller's side in the snappy yellow Kissel Kar, off to dinner, to the theatre, to the country, to parties. Under his influence she began to dress with greater care, to learn the social amenities.

"She receives instruction excellently, follows direction closely," he told a friend. "She is like wax in my hand."

Working with the raw material of a nature which only he at this time understood, Stiller gave artistic definition to Greta Gustafsson. At the completion of filming she wondered if she should not take a shorter, more international-sounding last name. Even here, Stiller was prepared. He toyed with Gabor, after Gabor Bethlen, an ancient Hungarian king, then settled on the variation, Garbo.

"I have had a Gethsemane," Greta said to a Swedish newspaperman, quickly adding, "but Stiller is the best human being I know. You never get angry or sad no matter how much he chastises you. He creates people and shapes them according to his will. As for myself, I am a nice girl who gets very sad if people are unkind to her, although that may not be very feminine. Being feminine is a lovely quality which I may not have very much of."

It is not surprising that at the beginning of her career Garbo should bring up the subject of femininity. In films to come she was often to display a considerable masculinity in dress and manner, and to exert an extraordinary sensual appeal for women as well as men. One story circulated later in Hollywood described a bridegroom on his wedding night who vowed that he would certainly be faithful—with one possible exception. If he had an opportunity to make love to Garbo, he would no doubt succumb. "Me too," said the unperturbed bride.

A certain sexual ambiguity emanated from Mauritz Stiller as well, an emotional man who would cry when extremely happy or sad. He was egotistic, narcissistic, artistic, a dandy; his complex nature included components often regarded as feminine. For those who responded to him, these were part of his attraction. Garbo responded: the powerful bond between her and Stiller was multifaceted, even mystical, interweaving the person and the profession, head and heart.

The Saga of Gösta Berling opened in Stockholm in March 1924, its running time four hours and ten minutes plus an intermission. Selma Lagerlof, annoyed at Stiller's fragmentation of her novel into a succession of major dramatic scenes, commented that he had seen too many serials. The public and most of the critics loudly applauded the work.

"If all but one Swedish silent film were to perish,

this, probably, would be the one to save as the best witness of its period. All the charm, intelligence, profound human resonance and technical dexterity here blend into an indissoluble bloc," French critic Jean Beranger has written.

The cast, including the newcomer in the second female lead, was praised, though not so extravagantly then as in later years. Commenting on a recent Garbo film festival, *Newsweek* reviewer Jack Kross wrote:

"In the climax . . . one is privileged to witness the birth of a deity. The accouchement occurs in a horse-drawn sled speeding across the ice pursued by a pack of ravenous wolves. Sweden's great star Lars Hanson, his eyes flashing Byronic fire, lashes the horses while the teen-age Garbo huddles terrified in her furs. Suddenly she looks up at Hanson in the first real Garbo close-up of all time, and there is the face of the goddess—her eyes, nose, mouth, chin, dimple palpitating in a Morse code of pure emotion. Stiller had painted his Mona Lisa."

The director's bargaining gift came to the fore when he sold the German rights to the film for a generous sum. After all was supposedly settled he squeezed out additional concessions, as was his usual pattern. The "extras" granted by the Trianon Film Company included an all-expense-paid trip to the Berlin premiere, not only for Stiller and Gerda Lundeqvist but for Greta Garbo. Also included were appropriate clothes for Garbo. Stiller chose them. They were expensive.

Stiller, who had a strong dislike of newspapermen, advised Greta to avoid them. It was better, he said, not to be readily available. She was turning into a star. A star should be distant, glimmer enticingly from afar.

At the Berlin premiere the film caused greater excitement than it had in Stockholm. Stiller rose in a box to acknowledge the applause. He shared the acclaim with his two female stars, one on either side.

"The German people are wonderful," Greta said at the time. "They do not touch you, yet they have their arms around you—always." In retrospect the remark is revealing. Throughout her life, Garbo was to seek out and inspire affection and love, never wishing it to be possessive. The American public was soon to put her through severe trials.

Stiller never completed another picture with his protégée. Intsead, a comic-opera adventure followed. Stiller signed with Trianon to direct another film, again exacting splendid terms. These concluded, he had afterthoughts. Trianon would also have to sign Greta Garbo. And young Einar Hanson, whom he had under contract. Then there was the matter of expenses. Finally, the German love story Trianon had in mind would not do at all. He, Stiller, would adapt a magazine story about the Crimean War. It dealt with a young girl who flees from Sevastopol on a Turkish barge hoping to meet her fiancé in Constantinople; she is sold into a harem by the crew, escapes, and eventually finds her sweetheart. Naturally the picture would be made in Turkey, for authenticity, and for economy in rounding up crowd scenes.

Trianon met the supersalesman's terms. Stiller and his entourage boarded the Orient express for Constantinople, on arrival checking into spacious quarters in the Pera Palace Hotel. It was December of 1924, close to Christmas. A large party for the city's Swedish colony was one of the first orders of business; hiring limousines with which to inspect location sites another. There was plenty of time. Weeks went by, happy hours occupied by shopping and sightseeing, visiting bazaars, walking quaint streets.

Stiller gave Greta a stunning fur coat, the traditional gift of the older gentleman admirer to his mistress. The two were often together, but Greta also liked to wander off by herself.

Stiller was finally ready to begin shooting when the money ran out. Imperiously he wired Trianon to send a million francs. There was no reply. He sent a second wire. No reply. Alone, he boarded the Orient Express for Berlin to chastise his derelict sponsors personally. His lecture to them was wasted: Trianon was bankrupt. The Swedish legation in Constantinople had to foot the bill for his troup's return.

Greta was unmoved by the debacle. Her trust in Stiller, who had handled all her contract negotiations, was complete—she was, after all, still a minor. Stiller himself sprinted away from disaster with the agility of an Olympic athlete. In Berlin he took a suite at the Tiergarten, where he also installed both Greta and Hanson. In fine spirits, he opened negotiations with various impresarios.

No firm offer came his way. G. W. Pabst, another gifted director, was about to make *The Joyless Street*, a realistic study of postwar decadence set in Vienna. To a cast which already included Werner Krauss and Danish actress Asta Nielsen, he wished to add Greta Garbo in the role of an elder daughter who tries to hold her family together. Stiller handled the terms, almost killing the deal with his demands—payment in American dollars, his own cameraman, living expenses, a role for Einar Hanson. Pabst agreed to everything except the camerman, insisting instead on Guido Seeber. Seeber handled Greta's facial twitch by speeding up the camera slightly, a technique which eliminated it. Pabst worked well with all his players—including Marlene Dietrich, who had a minor role—but the film's grim theme met with a mixed reception from audiences.

Stiller had coached Greta for the film. At the same time he was trying to organize a giant Continental film combine which would further both their careers. His grandiose plans fell through. Greta, meanwhile, was approached for another film by Pabst. She neglected to tell Stiller, who learned of the offer from Hanson. In a rage he accused her of betraying him. Greta first wept, then agreed to break off her talks with Pabst.

Stiller was already hatching another master plan. He learned that an important American movie magnate was coming to Berlin—Louis B. Mayer, a one-time junk dealer who had risen to vice president in charge of production for Metro-Goldwyn-Mayer, a studio which was soon to boast "more stars than there are in the heavens." Mayer had been to Rome to unsnarl problems besetting its multimillion-dollar production of *Ben Hur*. He was now touring the Continent in search of talent, following the pattern of other American studios which had already lured away artists like Pola Negri, Emil Jannings, Conrad Veidt, and Ernst Lubitsch. Mayer himself had Victor Seastrom under contract; with Stiller, Seastrom had guided the Swedish cinema to its position of international prominence.

Stiller wanted to meet Mayer, but he was shrewd. He arranged for an intermediary to beguile the production chief with extravagant talk of *Gösta Berling*. Mayer was impressed, saw the picture, and asked to meet the director. Stiller moved to the elegant Hotel Esplanade —a more impressive setting, he felt. Mayer came and made an offer; Stiller turned it down, then demanded the outsize sum of $1,500 a week. Mayer wired Seastrom in Hollywood and asked if Stiller was really that good. Seastrom's praise was lavish, and Mayer met Stiller's terms.

With this major point settled, the incorrigible Stiller attacked on a new front. Naturally, he said, he could not go to America unless Greta Garbo were also signed. Mayer explained that he had more than enough attractive girls already under contract at MGM. Stiller was immovable—he would not go without Greta. At least, then, he should meet her, said Mayer.

Garbo later described the encounter: "When I met Mr. Mayer, he hardly looked at me. All of the business was done with Mr. Stiller. Whatever Mr. Stiller said, I knew instinctively was always the best thing to do. I would say, 'Is it good?' and if he said 'It is good,' I would do it."

In order to get Stiller, Mayer signed Greta to a three-year contract, $350 per week for the first year, $600 the second, and $750 the third. He fired a parting shot when all was arranged: "Tell her that in America men don't like fat women."

Greta no doubt expected the streets of New York to be decked with flowers. They were not. When the Swedish liner *Drottningholm* docked at the Fifty-seventh Street pier on July 6, 1925, one solitary news photographer was on hand. He snapped a few pictures and that was that.

The two foreigners checked into the Commodore Hotel. New York was having one of its monstrous hot spells, and Greta spent a good deal of time cooling off in the bathtub. Occasionally she went window shopping, scandalized by the prices of goods.

Stiller, screenplays whirling in his mind, called MGM with a story idea. No one in the New York office seemed to be interested; Nicholas Schenck, the executive head, never found time for an appointment. It was humiliating treatment for a man who was a celebrity in Europe, accustomed to red-carpet receptions.

Stiller felt a great disdain for journalists, but he saw that something must be done. Alice Whitely Fletcher, editor of *Motion Picture Magazine*, recalls that at this time she received an SOS from a friend at Metro. Would she go over and interview a young Swedish actress? They did not expect her to use the material; they simply wanted her to create the illusion of activity.

"It will help us with Stiller. It will get him off our back," said her friend.

The editor went to the hotel, where Garbo, Stiller, and an interpreter awaited her. Greta was wearing a navy blue suit, not particularly well tailored, with a white blouse. She had taken off a coat and thrown it over a chair, seeking comfort above all else. She walked back and forth, her skirt riding up in the back, a strip of lingerie showing whenever she moved.

"What do you most want to do in New York?" asked the editor.

"I want to go to the Follies," Greta said assertively, almost belligerently. "I want to see if those girls are really beautiful. I want to see if they are any more beautiful than I am."

During this first interview in America, Greta was definite, frank, honest, refreshingly different from the typical vacuous Hollywood starlet. A few words about her appeared in the next issue of *Motion Picture*.

Occasionally Stiller and Greta would go to a movie or a play, carefully studying techniques despite their difficulties with the language. As the scorching days passed, they were tempted to break their contracts and return home. A Swedish friend took them to the studio of famed photographer Arnold Genthe. Struck by a poetic quality in Greta's face, he asked her to pose. He threw a simple gold sheath across her shoulder, brushed back her hair, and experimented with light and shadow. Genthe captured an essence others had overlooked, and a full-page photo from the sitting appeared in *Vanity Fair*. The others eventually caught the attention of an MGM executive, who gave orders to seek out the model with a view to signing her. There was considerable embarrassment when it was learned that Greta Garbo was already under contract to the studio.

At last, after three months in New York, the call came to move on to Hollywood. The reception at the railroad station was pleasant. Some twenty people were on hand—members of the Swedish colony; Joseph Polansky, head of foreign publicity for MGM, one of the first studios to have such a department; photographer Don Gillum; several reporters; and a little Swedish girl under contract to Metro—Louis B. Mayer liked child stars. This one handed a bouquet of flowers to a smiling Greta as the cameras clicked.

Further afflictions were in store for the newcomers, however. Hollywood was used to "It" girl Clara Bow and the other flappers; to glamorous Gloria Swanson; to the refined Norma Shearer; to Lillian Gish, ever fighting for her honor. Most of the reigning female stars were women with soft little mouths and dainty hands and feet. Tall, angular Greta went against the standard grain. Her ascent was to lead to Alexis Smith and Ingrid Bergman and Ava Gardner, but their day was still far off.

A screen test left studio executives indifferent. Stiller protested angrily because he was not brought in. He insisted on making another, and this time he both supervised the makeup and coached Greta. This second effort impressed Mayer and his gifted right hand Irving Thalberg more favorably.

The publicity department was now called into action. Its head, Pete Smith, alerted Don Gillum and Larry Barbier, head of the publicity art department. Gillum, who had studied at the University of Southern California, knew there were three Swedes on the football team and another on the track team. He took Greta to the campus, asked her to put on a track suit, and posed her at the starting line with coach Dean Cromwell and his men.

Another day, Gillum took Greta to the beach. The shots of her gamboling in the sand could not be used;

they showed that she wore nothing underneath her suit.

When the early photos were picked up by the press, Stiller, who felt they were cheap and undignified, stormed about the MGM lot.

"No more pictures of this Swedish dame," Pete Smith now told his staff. "She's been complaining to Stiller and Stiller's been complaining to Mayer. Talk to me before you do anything more with her."

The studio reassessed the situation. No one knew what kind of image Greta should be made to convey. During several interviews reporters found her uncommunicative. She belittled her own opinions, which therefore were ignored—except for complaints that "Everything is so big here." Louis B. Mayer took offense, assuming Greta meant that MGM was too commercial, not a true dispenser of art. Another of her remarks perturbed him even more.

"Where do you plan to make your home?" asked a reporter.

"I would like to live with some nice private family," said Greta.

Mayer had a firm concept of what a star should be. Stars were fabulous creatures—workaday mortals could look up to them because they drank champagne instead of beer, ate caviar rather than hamburgers, were not concerned with mundane matters. Mayer gave orders that Greta was not to see reporters unless a studio agent went along to guide her. Reporters, said Greta, would intimidate her. Mayer offered her a choice: the presence of a studio aide or no more interviews. She chose the latter, but not before one crucial article broke into print.

"In America you are all so happy," Greta said to

journalist Rilla Page Palmborg. "Why are you happy all the time? Sometimes yes, sometimes no. I am not always happy."

"Always," an important word in her observation, was overlooked. In the land of Coolidge prosperity a foreign actress was apparently questioning the spirit of the people. Her attitude was puzzling to her interviewer, who entitled her magazine piece "The Mysterious Stranger" and concluded it with a sentence which was to give a powerful thrust to the Garbo mystique: "Greta Garbo will fascinate people, but I wager she will always remain more or less a mystery."

"I told Garbo that mystery had served me well and it would do as much for her," Lon Chaney said years later. "She is a clever woman and she adopted my policy of never having portraits made except in character and never giving interviews—and look where it carried her!"

Whatever the provocation, such epithets as "The Enigmatic Swede," "The Swedish Sphinx," and "The Mysterious Stranger" were soon applied to Greta by promotion writers and an acquiescent press.

Meanwhile Greta moved into the Miramar, a small hotel in Santa Monica; Stiller rented a bungalow near the beach. They were often together—adrift, confused, unhappy. Their best moments were at the homes of other members of the Swedish colony—the Seastroms, or Lars Hanson, or interior designer Erich Stocklossa. Here they could relax. Greta particularly enjoyed playing with the children. With them she seemed more comfortable than with adults.

Stiller was becoming increasingly frustrated. One evening he left a director's house and tapped the column at the entrance. "You see, hollow," he said. "That's why they call it Hollowwood. . . . The only way to impress people in this country is by not being impressed."

Stiller's greatest humiliation came when Garbo was finally assigned to a film and he was not put in charge. For the man who, at considerable risk, had tied his own career to that of his protégée, it was a bitter blow.

Monta Bell, a director of modest program films, was given *The Torrent*, adapted from the novel by Blasco Ibañez. Stiller coached and rehearsed Greta each night.

"If she's a success, I'll give you the finest watch you've ever seen," said skeptical Louis B. Mayer.

Before filming began, Mayer ordered Greta's teeth fixed—there was too much space between them—and also demanded that she lose weight. She dieted rigidly. This, and the long hours of work, from six in the morning until six at night, sapped her strength.

Used to more intimate conditions in small European studios, Greta was awed by the elaborate factory atmosphere at MGM. She had difficulty understanding Monta Bell's direction, voiced in English or expressed through an interpreter. At the same time, Greta's knowledge of the language was beginning to grow and she was able to feel the insulting brunt of phrases like "What makes that big Swede think she can act?" "Tell that dumb Swede we're ready to start shooting," and "Where the hell's the flatfoot?"

Ricardo Cortez, billed as the star of *The Torrent*, was clearly displeased at having an unknown co-star. In one scene, where both came out of the water, Greta's maid held out a blanket to dry her. Cortez expropriated it. "Never mind, he is only a pumpkin," said Greta, having found a word she thought described his pomposity and presumption.

Things began looking up for her long before the completion of the picture. The early rushes startled Irving Thalberg and Mayer. In repose, sitting with her shoulders stooped, her eyes half closed, Greta seemed devoid of allure. Then would come the call before the cameras. She would rise with a movement of astonishing grace and suddenly the face would come to life, its haunting beauty apparent to all. Hers was a love affair with the camera.

Monta Bell saw what was happening. Even the grips were aware that a star was in the making. Mayer called Greta to his office and said he wanted to renegotiate her contract—upwards. Greta said no, she would rather wait. Mayer looked at her with dismay and an awakening of respect. They should rethink the matter of publicity, he said. Metro was going to make her an international celebrity and there should be a proper publicity campaign, a big buildup, photos, endorsements, perhaps a Garbo soap or a Garbo something else.

"No, I don't think so," said Greta.

"We're spending all this money on you," pursued Mayer. "Don't you think you should cooperate?"

"Wouldn't it be cheaper to make a good movie?" she asked. There, for the moment, the matter ended.

The Swedish colony, especially Stiller, thought the final version of *The Torrent* terrible. The critics, largely ignoring Cortez, hailed a new star. *Variety* pronounced Greta the find of the year and said, "This girl has everything, with looks, acting ability, and personality." In the New York *Herald Tribune*, Richard Watts Jr.

said: "She seems an excellent and attractive actress with a surprising propensity for looking like Carol Dempster, Norma Talmadge, Zasu Pitts, and Gloria Swanson in turn. That does not mean she lacks a manner of her own, however."

"She registers a complete success," wrote the critic for *Motion Picture*. "She is not so much an actress as she is endowed with individuality and magnetism."

More good news came with the announcement that Stiller would direct her second picture, *The Temptress*, again based on a Blasco Ibañez novel. Only swift disaster lay ahead. Stiller wanted to turn the standard story of a man-enslaving vamp into a richly embroidered spectacle. And he wanted to film it in his own manner. He ordered MGM's vast echelons of production assistants off the film. He began shooting, not in sequence but as the spirit moved him, as he had done in Europe. Thalberg looked at the rushes and could make no sense out of the jumbled images. He wondered if he was dealing with another Erich Von Stroheim, who had just made a version of the Frank Norris novel, *McTeague*. Called *Greed*, it ran fifty reels, eight hours' running time, and cost a sizable fortune above budget.

Stiller's eccentric personality and techniques became the laughingstock and the dismay of executives. He was a dictator on the lot, ordering publicity people away with Swedish, German, and Slavic imprecations. He had learned "Hallo" from telephone usage and thought he could get action at any moment by using that term. At other times he would try to start the cameras by shouting "Stop," or to stop them with the command "Go." When he wanted applause, he bellowed "Explode!"

Leading man Antonio Moreno was a problem. Stiller stirred his Latin temper by ordering him to shave a prized moustache. He further insisted that he wear boots several sizes too large in order to make Greta's feet appear smaller. When he asked Moreno to style his hair in a pompadour because Garbo was so tall, Moreno balked. After several weeks of turmoil, Thalberg removed the harassed director and replaced him with Fred Niblo, who had rescued *Ben Hur*.

Shortly thereafter, Greta received word that her sister Alva had died of tuberculosis. The combination of factors—exhaustion, her sister's death, and Stiller's dismissal—depressed her greatly, but she finished the picture. The chorus of acclaim was headed by Robert Sherwood in *Life:*

"I want to go on record as saying that Greta Garbo in *The Temptress* knocked me for a loop. . . . She may not be the best actress on the screen—I am powerless to formulate an opinion on her dramatic technique—but there is no room for argument as to the efficacy of her allure."

The deflated Stiller asked to be released from his contract. He was allowed to go to Paramount, where his old friend Erich Pommer had asked for him. There Stiller made the story MGM had rejected. As *Hotel Imperial*, with Pola Negri, it was a welcome triumph. Two lesser efforts followed, and then came arguments with Paramount executives. Hollywood could not easily accept Stiller's theories, and his nature allowed little compromise.

His career lagging, Stiller now found his health breaking down. In his madcap manner he had gone out one night poorly dressed; then, thinking it would buoy his health, he went swimming in the cold winter ocean. He contracted a painful case of rheumatism which was to trouble him the rest of his days.

Dejected, Stiller sailed for home in 1927. Garbo and Stiller embraced, and wept, and said goodbye. They were never to see each other again.

In Stockholm Stiller directed a musical play, *Broadway*, and regained some of his old-time exuberance, only to fall severely ill of a combination of ailments. Victor Seastrom returned to Sweden and visited him daily. He has recalled their poignant last meeting, when Stiller made idle chatter until the nurse said he must rest:

"Then suddenly Stiller got desperate," Seastrom said. "He grabbed my arm in despair and would not let me go. 'No, no,' he cried. 'I haven't told him what I must tell him!' The nurse separated us and pushed me toward the door. I tried to quiet and comfort him, saying that he could tell it to me tomorrow. But he got more and more desperate. His face was wet with tears. And he said, 'I want to tell you a story for a film. It will be a great film. It is about real human beings, and you are the only one who can do it.'

"I was so moved I didn't know what to say. 'I will be with you the first thing in the morning and then you can tell me,' I said. I left him crying in the arms of the nurse. There was no morning."

Stiller, only forty-five, died that night. It is interesting to speculate about the story he so longed to tell his friend, the story about "real people" which he kept painfully to himself until the last. Perhaps it was the account of a great director and his love for a young actress.

Greta Garbo was playing a love scene with Nils Asther in *Wild Orchids* when they brought her the telegram. She turned pale, looked faint, walked to a corner and leaned against a wall, hands pressed to her eyes. Then, without a word, she returned to continue the scene.

"I have Mauritz Stiller to thank for everything in the world," she had once said. And, on another occasion: "If I were ever to love anyone, it would be Mauritz Stiller."

Did Greta Garbo actually love Stiller? There were recurrent reports from middle-European capitals that the two had been secretly married. Such rumors were never denied by either. Unlike other celebrities, Garbo has seldom denied anything said about her, a habit which has added to her mystery and made it more difficult to disentangle truth from fiction.

An author friend states that he worked for years with Garbo on her autobiography, that Stiller was the obsession of her life, that there was a child which died at the age of five. At the time of Stiller's departure for home, he reportedly begged Greta to come with him. She asked permission of MGM to break her contract but was told no. She stayed and Stiller went, leaving her only with sad memories and guilt. In 1964, when this autobiography was finally completed, Garbo withdrew permission to have it published. There were too many frank revelations, she felt, and now was not the time to air them.

Several writers have speculated about Stiller's reaction to Garbo's sensationally publicized affair with John Gilbert. There are those who have said they were intense rivals, that Stiller broke up prospective marriage plans between Garbo and Gilbert, that Gilbert was intensely jealous of Stiller, that in turn Stiller was heartbroken by Garbo's defection. Before Stiller's death, Gilbert, asked what he thought Garbo wanted in life, said:

"What does she want to do? I know better than she does, I suppose. She wants to work with Stiller. After all, he was her first friend and her first god. Stiller discovered her. He taught her to act, and he understood her. He knows what she is up against. She can be happy with Stiller. I don't think I was ever Stiller's real rival with Greta."

It was a remarkable confession for the dashing, vainglorious actor.

In December of 1929, having made eight films in three years, a worn-out Greta returned to visit her home in Sweden. She asked about Stiller's grave and made an appointment to meet one of his friends from happier days. At the street corner fixed for their rendezvous she saw the friend approaching. Suddenly she turned and left, unable to face the encounter. While in Sweden, she went to see Stiller's possessions shortly before they were to be sold at auction. The estate's executor who accompanied her noted the way she touched the objects, caressing them and recalling where they came from. Friends who have seen her in recent years say that when Garbo walks into a room she touches the things she likes.

For years, Greta often spoke of Stiller as if he were alive, referring to something Moje—her pet name for him—would have said or done. Friends found this evocation of her "first god" strangely touching. Gradually, the references to Moje grew less frequent.

Today, Greta Garbo lives in a New York apartment with seven rooms, four of which are empty. Only the L-shaped living room is completely furnished. She had been in the apartment for several years when one of her friends asked designer William Baldwin to help her with the decoration of the bedroom. Baldwin came to inspect and worked out a plan. During its execution, he had occasion to see the one other room in the house with any furniture. All alone in solitary splendor stood the most beautiful piece in the apartment, a pale cream-toned table, seventeenth-century Scandinavian.

"This looks more like you than anything else," said Baldwin.

The table, bought by Garbo at auction, had come from the estate of Mauritz Stiller.

Garbo and Gilbert

Although the Garbo mystique has adequately expressed her need to escape the glare of publicity, it has always failed to reflect the diversity in her private life outside the limelight. In Hollywood, Garbo, always moody, sometimes suffered depressions, looked at the world with gloomy eyes, kept to herself; she also experienced periods of elation, participated in at least an average share of romances, and formed long and meaningful friendships. She knew, in fact, an extraordinary number of people over the years, most of them highly gifted and outgoing. If Garbo was a hermit, she was surely the most gregarious hermit of her time.

Her affair with John Gilbert, one of the most widely ballyhooed of all screen liaisons, illustrates her remarkable ability to go out into the world with frequency while simultaneously investing herself with mystery and an appearance of loneliness and isolation.

Greta was twenty-one when she met Gilbert, eight years her senior. The product of a broken home and an impoverished childhood, he had gone into films hoping to direct; his sleek matinee-idol appearance put him into demand as an actor. He made a number of unimportant pictures, then came under Erich Von Stroheim's direction in 1925. The film was *The Merry Widow*. Von Stroheim told Gilbert he was a foul artist, which made him so angry that he turned in a fiery performance. *The Merry Widow*, co-starring Mae Murray, was an enormous success.

Gilbert followed it with the role of doughboy Jim Apperson in *The Big Parade*, and next played opposite Lillian Gish in *La Bohème*. By 1926 he was earning $10,000 a week as one of the leading male stars of the silent screen, higher paid than Rudolph Valentino. He was described at the time as dynamic, unpredictable, tempestuous, high-strung, gay, generous, convivial, reckless, grandiloquent, and mad. Obviously, he was the perfect companion for a recluse.

When MGM decided to pair him with Greta in *Flesh and the Devil* Gilbert's stature far surpassed hers; she had made only two American pictures. Notwithstanding the career opportunity, she looked askance at the thought of playing another vamp. For two days she stayed at home to think it over before consenting to start filming. Once shooting had begun, the results were electric. Gilbert, with his coal-black hair and flashing dark eyes, vibrated to the tall, blond Greta, equally intense in her own way.

"I am working with raw material," director Clarence Brown said with obvious delight. "They are in that blissful state of love so like a rosy cloud that they imagine themselves hidden behind it, as well as lost in it."

Brown watched, fascinated, as the screen story unfolded. It was his distinct impression that Greta and Gilbert were privately living its counterpart, their real love developing even as the cameras rolled. At times they responded so tardily to his order to cut that he and the technicians felt like eavesdroppers.

The studio was enchanted by the comments of Brown and others on the filming, for each item was snapped up by the press and fed to an insatiable public. When Greta began to be seen with Gilbert in his snappy roadster, zipping down the boulevard, up to his mansion high on Tower Road overlooking Beverly Hills, and dining in the dark recesses of restaurants, the pandemonium was complete. The critics were so preconditioned that when *Flesh and the Devil* appeared they were like fuses ready to ignite—and indeed the film's open-mouth kisses were a daring innovation at the time.

"Here is a picture that is the pay-off when it comes to filming love scenes. There are three in this picture that will make anyone fidget in their seat and their hair rise on end," said *Variety*.

"Never before has John Gilbert been so intense in his portrayal of a man in love," said the New York *Herald Tribune*. "Never before has a woman so alluring, with a seductive grace that is far more potent than mere beauty, appeared on the screen. Greta Garbo is the epitome of pulchritude, the personification of passion. . . . Frankly, never have we seen seduction so perfectly done."

Flesh and the Devil, catapulted into a publicity orgy by the romance with Gilbert, made Greta an important star. In three successive films she had managed to inject fresh life into a characterization generally considered shopworn, that of the vamp who leads men to their destruction but is herself weary and marked for doom. The time-tried Hollywood formula was to repeat what had succeeded before, but MGM was reckoning without Greta. Throughout her career she was to fight for solid story material. When the studio saddled her with a script called *Women Love Diamonds*, she failed to show for costume fittings. She wanted to play "no more bad womens," she explained on the phone.

Louis B. Mayer, well on the road to becoming the most powerful man in Hollywood, was furious. A letter which arrived at the Miramar stated that Greta was breaking her contract by not appearing at the studio. MGM, therefore, was under no obligation to pay her salary.

Salary was indeed not far from Greta's mind. She was getting $600 a week against Gilbert's $10,000. When Mayer called her into his office, she brought the matter up. What did she have in mind, he asked.

"Five thousand dollars a week," she said quietly.

Mayer offered her half.

"I tank I go home," said Greta, and went.

The remark set into motion one of the most cele-brated contract disputes of Hollywood's golden age. For seven months Greta went into retreat at the Mira-mar. The studio let out the threatening news that as an unemployed alien she would have difficulty renewing her passport. This troubled her little, for Stiller was still around, and miserable, and thinking about going home anyhow. And Gilbert, himself at war with producers, was encouraging her to wring every penny out of them.

He introduced her to a man who was to be a stabi-
lizing force in her life—Harry Edington, one of Hollywood's first business managers. His career had begun
in the accounting department of MGM, a spot which
gave him a valuable insight into studio costs. In 1924 he
went to Rome to watch over production charges on
Ben Hur, and on his return set up his own firm. His
first client was producer Carey Wilson. Wilson led him
to Gilbert, for whom he brilliantly negotiated a million-
dollar contract.

Greta was by now eager for activity, as was Gilbert,
whom the studio was holding in reserve for her. MGM,
watching her early films bring in fantastic foreign
grosses, was soon ready to negotiate. Edington, handling
Greta as a prestige client without charging commission,
spent the better part of a week with studio executives.
He emerged holding a five-year contract that justifiably
satisfied her. Her starting salary was $5,000 per week,
scaled up to $6,000 a week in the fifth year. Moreover,
she was to be paid not the usual forty weeks annually
but the entire fifty-two.

Neither Mayer nor Greta could have foreseen that
the holdout would give an almighty boost to the legend
of Greta Garbo the sphinx, the aloof, the mysterious.
Or that as this legend grew, her box-office value would
spiral. Edington is generally credited with supplying the
grace note to this powerful double thrust. Henceforth,
he said, like other performers of the highest stature, she
should be known by a single name—Garbo.

For Garbo, John Gilbert was a link to a new life,
and his buoyancy carried her with him. He was no

intellectual, but he courted literary lights and people in the arts, as well as the more sophisticated screen personalities. There were Sunday brunches and social evenings with screenwriter Herman Mankiewicz and his wife Sarah, author-journalist Adela Rogers St. Johns, producers Carey Wilson and Arthur Hornblow Jr., writers Louis Bromfield, S. N. Behrman, and Sidney Howard.

Gilbert introduced them all to Garbo, who was always responsive to people who could supplement her limited formal education. She had to be in the right mood to meet new people, however. One day she was playing tennis with actress Aileen Pringle when she heard the front bell. Aileen explained that she was expecting a friend, author Carl Van Vechten, a man she would enjoy. Garbo's face froze and she said no, she would not meet him. Aileen explained to Van Vechten, who waited patiently until the tennis game was over. Later, he and Aileen sat on the terrace talking and drinking while Garbo waited inside for her chauffeur, unable to go through the ordeal of meeting a new person.

Once Gilbert had drawn her into his circle, meeting people became less difficult for Garbo. She even came to enjoy Gilbert's flamboyance. In the tradition of a true star, he lived each screen role. When he played a Cossack, he dismissed half his staff and replaced them with expatriate Russians whom he dressed in colorful native costumes. Vodka and caviar were soon in evidence, and a balalaika orchestra played during evening meals.

His overall screen characterization was that of the great lover, and as a consequence romance became an afterwork preoccupation. He had already been married to starlet Mary Hay and to Leatrice Joy, prominent on stage and screen. Both marriages ended in divorce. He had courted many others, including Dorothy Parker, before beginning his impetuous pursuit of Garbo. When he was not taking her to friends' houses, he escorted her to restaurants, drove her out for picnics, or coaxed her up to his hilltop house for swimming or sunbathing. He ordered an entire wing of the house redecorated for her. When she saw the black marble bathroom on which he had spent a fortune, her only comment was that it was too shiny. Workmen came in and started anew.

Garbo's candor both charmed and infuriated Gilbert. As with everyone else, she was maddeningly unpredictable, reluctant to make plans in advance, changing them at the last minute. There were quarrels, which led to memorable days in the Gilbert household.

"If Miss Garbo calls, I'm not in," he would advise his servants.

"Did Miss Garbo call?" he would inquire an hour later. "Remember, I'm not in."

At the end of the day he would make one last inquiry and then reverse his field: "Get Miss Garbo on the phone."

In his public pronouncements, which were as regular and frequent as medical bulletins on an ailing monarch, Gilbert further helped build the Garbo mystique.

"Garbo is marvelous," he said in a typical rhapsody. "The most alluring creature you have ever seen. Capricious as the devil, whimsical, temperamental and fascinating. Some days she refuses to come to the studio. When she doesn't feel like working, she will *not* work. Garbo never acts unless she feels she can do herself justice. But what magnetism when she gets in front of the camera! What appeal! What a woman! One day she is childlike, naive, ingenuous, a girl of ten. The next day she is a mysterious woman a thousand years old, knowing everything, baffling, deep. Garbo has more sides to her personality than anyone I have ever met."

Gilbert proposed many times and at least twice thought he was close to the altar. On one occasion he persuaded Garbo to elope to Mexico. In Santa Ana he made the mistake of stopping for lunch. There she suddenly bolted, some said because she feared Stiller was on their trail. She fled to a nearby hotel and locked herself in the ladies' room, later taking a train back to Hollywood by herself.

Another time Gilbert bought a two-masted sailing schooner with the intention of taking her on a honeymoon cruise to the South Seas. In Garbo's honor he named the boat *The Temptress*, and spent a small fortune putting her into shape. For the first outing he invited King Vidor, Irving Thalberg, and Norma Shearer on an excursion to the nearby island of Catalina. As they inspected the ship, the guests kept looking for Garbo. The elusive star was in one of her private moods. When the party moved forward she slipped into the crew's quarters, then evaded them again when they were aft, keeping one step ahead. Once Norma thought she caught a glimpse of Garbo, but they never met. Shortly after this fiasco, Gilbert sold the boat.

Adela Rogers St. Johns saw a good deal of Gilbert during these and later years, and he became the godfather of her youngest son. One afternoon they discussed Garbo.

"She says she'll marry if I will let her retire from the screen," Gilbert said. "She hates acting. She hates Hollywood and everything in it. She wants to buy half of Montana or whatever state has no people in it and turn it into a wheat farm and raise wheat and children. She keeps saying, 'You're in love with Garbo the actress.' And you know, I say, 'You damn right.' Frankly, I don't want to marry some dumb Swede and raise wheat and have kids miles from civilization."

"She never in all the time I knew her talked of herself," he said on another occasion. For the effusive Gilbert, Garbo's holding back, her guarding a part of herself even in romance, was hard to take; to her, he must often have seemed an impetuous child, not to be taken too seriously.

When Stiller, in an interlude between films, spent an evening with Garbo, Gilbert took one drink too many and arrived brandishing a revolver. Later, police stopped his car as he was speeding down Wilshire Boulevard and locked him up for the night in the Beverly Hills jail. Gilbert had had enough. He headed for New York, announcing that he and Garbo were "just pals."

The public devoured every scrap of news about the teeter-tottering romance, which extended over two years and three films: *Flesh and the Devil; Love,* a version of Tolstoy's *Anna Karenina* cleverly retitled so that the advertisements could read "Greta Garbo and John Gilbert in *Love*"; and *A Woman of Affairs,* adapted from Michael Arlen's popular novel *The Green Hat.*

Garbo was constantly solicited for comments on the relationship and on love and marriage. "Love?" she said

at one time to Ake Sundborg, "Well, it is the beginning
and the ending of a woman's education. How can one
express love if one has never experienced it? Marriage?
I have said over and over again that I do not know.
There is always my overwhelming desire to be alone."

To Rilla Page Palmborg she gave her only specific
comment on Gilbert: "Many things have been written
and said about our friendship. It is a friendship. I will
never marry, but you may say that I think John Gilbert
is one of the finest men I have ever known. He has
temperament, he gets excited. Sometimes he has much
to say, but that is good. I am very happy when I am
told that I am to do a picture with Mr. Gilbert. He is
a great artist. He lifts me up and carries me along with
him. It is not scenes I am doing—I am living."

By the time of *A Woman of Affairs* in 1929 the
romance was over, and Garbo allegedly said, "God, I
wonder what I ever saw in him. Oh, well, I guess he was
pretty." She cautioned director Clarence Brown about
the love scenes and murmured, "Turn backward, turn
backward, oh time in thy flight."

Gilbert, after his ardor had cooled, was gallant. "She
is a mountain of a girl. She is like a statue," he said.
"There is something eternal about her. Not only did
she baffle me but she baffled everyone at the studio.
Once, she had been missing for days and I went to see
her. Her maid told me she had gone to the beach. I
jumped in my car and motored for miles way out beyond Santa Monica. I found her at last. She was all
alone and just coming out of the surf. She didn't see
me so I watched her to see what she would do. She

stood on the beach all by herself and just looked out at the ocean for fifteen minutes. And that's when she's really happy—standing alone watching the ocean."

A number of Gilbert's friends were ready to predict the break-up, and they saw it as equally his decision. Fredric March recalls an occasion when Garbo was returning from a trip out of town.

"Aren't you going to meet the train?" he asked.

"No," said Gilbert. "She may be Garbo, but I'm still Jack Gilbert."

When Gilbert married Ina Claire in 1929, one paper headed its story GARBO COLLAPSES AS GILBERT MARRIES and placed it above an unrelated item that read BEAUTY TRIES TO END HER LIFE. Garbo was asked to comment. "Oh, it's so silly," she said.

A decade later Ina Claire joined Garbo in the cast of *Ninotchka* and the two became good friends. By this time Garbo was insisting on closed sets, but stagehands who adored Ina Claire let her peek through holes for one moving scene in which the arrival of flowers elicits the first feminine emotion in the Communist diplomat played by Garbo.

"Are you ready, Miss Garbo?" asked the director.

"As soon as Miss Claire gets from behind that curtain, yes," said Garbo, who had an uncanny instinct for detecting an unauthorized presence.

The stagehands moved Ina to a better concealed location, and this time she saw the scene. "Well, I am here to tell you that scene was one of the most extraordinary things I've ever seen," she told Garbo when it was over. "And damn you, I saw you cry."

"Very unmanly of me, wasn't it?" said Garbo, and returned to her dressing room.

The epilogue to the Gilbert-Garbo affair was both touching and tragic. His marriage to Ina Claire ended in divorce, as did a fourth excursion into matrimony with beautiful Virginia Bruce. While Garbo's career continued its dizzying climb, Gilbert's plummeted. The advent of sound was a main cause.

When the talkies came in, MGM was worried about Garbo's accent rather that Gilbert's voice. They delayed her entry into the new medium as long as possible, making *The Kiss* as a silent film in late 1929, MGM's last. At the time of Garbo's first talkie, *Anna Christie*, the studio blanketed the country with the slogan "Garbo talks!" Even then, director Clarence Brown held back the momentous event for thirty-four minutes, well into the second reel. Audiences applauded the sensual, throaty voice which finally uttered those memorable words, "Gimme a whisky. Chinger ale on the side. An' don' be stingy, babee."

No such good fortune greeted Gilbert. Imperfect sound machinery brought forth his voice as high-pitched and thin. He made *Redemption*, adapted from Tolstoy's *The Living Corpse*, but it was so bad that the studio shelved it, reworked it, and held up the release date for almost a year. In the meantime Gilbert made *His Glorious Night*, adapted from Molnar's *Olympia* and directed by Lionel Barrymore. The great lover's first line of dialogue was, unfortunately, "I love you, I love you, I love you." Audiences greeted the shrill tenor tones with jeers and laughter.

Early in his career Gilbert had exhibited a flair for comedy, but once the mantle of the great lover began to envelop him he was given no opportunity to put it aside. In comic roles, his voice might well have been an asset.

Gilbert's career was sadly on the wane in 1933 when Garbo was about to make *Queen Christina*, the story of Sweden's eccentric, fascinating seventeenth-century monarch. Ricardo Cortez, Fredric March, Franchot Tone, and Nils Asther were tested for the leading male role and rejected. The part was finally given to young English actor Laurence Olivier, who has told the story of how he lost it at the first rehearsal scene:

"The stage was set for our most important scene when, as Don Antonio, I meet Garbo in her boudoir at the inn and there discover the warm, tender woman beneath the boyish masquerade. And this is the part of my story I shall always look back upon with a mixture of amazement and disappointment. The director explained that I was to come forward, grasp Garbo's slender body tenderly, look into her eyes and, in the gesture, awaken passion within her, that passion for which she is later willing to give up the Swedish throne. I went into my role giving it everything I had, but at the touch of my hand Garbo became frigid. I could feel the sudden tautness of her, her eyes as stony and expressionless as if she were marble."

Director Rouben Mamoulian made every effort to overcome Garbo's incapacity to register emotion with Olivier. He failed. To everyone's astonishment, Garbo went to see Louis B. Mayer and asked for John Gilbert. Mayer held out for a time. While waiting for the role to be recast, Garbo was scheduled to shoot scenes not involving the male lead. She sent word that she was ill. Mayer got the message, and Gilbert got the role.

Queen Christina won great critical acclaim, but it was Garbo's performance that everyone praised. Gilbert was largely ignored, and his career continued its decline. For this he blamed Mayer, toward whom he developed an almost pathological hatred.

"Where are you going?" Adela Rogers St. Johns asked Gilbert one day when she saw him backing his car much too speedily out of an alley in Malibu.

"I'm going to kill Louis B. Mayer."

"They'll hang you."

"No, I'll kill him and then myself."

"Take me with you. You shouldn't be alone on a mission like this. Besides, you can't drive in this condition. You've been drinking."

"I have to kill that sonofabitch or I can't live in the world."

Adela eventually talked Gilbert out of this highly emotional state, but in a sense Gilbert did proceed to kill himself. It was humiliating for a man with his ego to accept the charitable offer of a role from Garbo—and then to be ignored. Thereafter, Gilbert made one more mediocre film, *The Captain Hates the Sea*. He now drank too much and drove too fast; soon he began psychiatric treatment.

Director Lewis Milestone, his close friend in the last years, remembers that it was Columbia's Harry Cohn, probably the most widely disliked studio head in Hollywood, who extended a helping hand. "Jack, if you behave and stay on the wagon, the world can be yours here at Columbia," he said.

Gilbert tried. He began a picture with Milestone, but after less than a week he broke down and was taken off the film. Bitter, broke, alone, he died of a heart attack in 1936. He was thirty-eight years old.

From Garbo there was no comment.

Hollywood Revisited

THE MAKING OF A STAR is both a matter of luck and of design. Physically, Garbo posed minor problems; she also brought to the process incalculable assets.

Each department at MGM was headed by an expert acknowledged to be at the top of his field. These men remolded Garbo, changing not the essence but the contours, sharpening, refining. Slimming down the body and perfecting the teeth were basic steps. The makeup department exercised its artistry, though later Garbo herself did what little was needed. While privately she preferred turtlenecks, plain skirts or slacks, and flat-heeled shoes, in films she became a style-setter. Gilbert Adrian, head of the studio's costume department, put her into long-sleeved, high-necked gowns that set off her best features. He invented a series of hats which women everywhere copied. Over the years many of his creations for Garbo became international high fashion.

Once sound came in, the man in charge was Norma Shearer's brother Douglas, who won Oscars year after year for his fine work. In every department there was continuity in the team working on Garbo pictures, from grips and gaffers to film editors and cameramen, and on up through the executive ranks.

Once she was back in the fold after the long-drawn-out contract dispute, Mayer and Thalberg readily acknowledged that Garbo was one of their richest assets. They surrounded her with elaborate and expensive settings (solidifying a process already underway before the dispute). The top leading men came her way—John Gilbert, Conrad Nagel, Nils Asther, Charles Bickford, Robert Montgomery, Ramon Novarro, Clark Gable, Melvyn Douglas, John Barrymore, Herbert Marshall, George Brent, Fredric March, Robert Taylor, and Charles Boyer—along with first-rung supporting casts.

Clarence Brown, responsible for many of MGM's other big pictures, directed seven Garbo films: *Flesh and the Devil*, *A Woman of Affairs*, *Anna Christie*, *Romance*, *Inspiration*, *Anna Karenina*, and *Conquest*. Other well-known directors were called in, sometimes at Garbo's request. Englishman Edmund Goulding was at the helm for *Love*, and skillfully brought home the all-star classic *Grand Hotel*. Garbo asked for, and got, Victor Seastrom as her director in *The Divine Woman*. Fred Niblo directed *The Mysterious Lady* and took over *The Temptress*. Jacques Feyder, one of France's finest film-makers, turned a trifle called *The Kiss* into something worthwhile through his use of evocative settings and lights. George Fitzmaurice directed *Mata Hari* and the Pirandello adaptation *As You Desire Me*. Robert Z. Leonard, Mae Murray's husband and director, did *Susan Lenox: Her Fall and Rise*. Rouben Mamoulian, a film innovator, made *Queen Christina.* George Cukor directed *Camille,* considered Garbo's best film by many critics, and *Two-Faced Woman,* universally considered her worst. And Ernst Lubitsch gave his distinctive touch to *Ninotchka.*

Metro bought popular and expensive properties for Garbo, works by Blasco Ibañez, Herman Sudermann, Michael Arlen, Edward Sheldon, and Vicki Baum, and dipped into classics and semiclassics for inspiration— Tolstoy, Dumas, Pirandello, Maugham, O'Neill. Highly paid writers and scenarists were put to work, among others Frances Marion, Bess Meredyth, Salka Viertel, Zoë Akins, S. N. Behrman, Charles Brackett, Billy Wilder, James Hilton, George Oppenheimer, and Adela Rogers St. Johns.

Metro demonstrated its readiness to spend extravagantly on its showcase star during her fourth film, *Love.* Russian-born Dmitri Buchowetzky was originally assigned to direct. Ricardo Cortez was the star, supported, among others, by Lionel Barrymore. From the beginning there were language and other difficulties with the director and problems of temperament with the stars. On seeing the early rushes, studio heads were dissatisfied. They decided to scrap the footage, replace Buchowetzky with Edmund Goulding and Cortez with John Gilbert, for whom the fans were clamoring. Lionel Barrymore also was sacrificed. The cost of this shifting of forces was nearly a quarter of a million dollars.

MGM may not always have acted or chosen wisely for Garbo, but it was certainly unstinting in its use of money and other resources. Everyone seemed to care. One wonders what would have happened if she had fallen into the hands of economy-minded "Uncle Carl" Laemmle at Universal. He might have put her into a serial.

As Garbo moved into national prominence, distortions and paradoxes evolved along with the legend. Perhaps the most ridiculous one concerns her feet. Early in the day Walter Winchell, one of the era's most widely syndicated columnists, printed an item saying that Garbo had large feet. The nation breathed sighs of relief as it learned that the goddess had not merely an Achilles heel but two whole big feet of clay.

The truth is more interesting. Rather than wear tight-fitting designer shoes on the set, Garbo walked around in roomy fluffy, low-heeled slippers—she liked to be comfortable. Warmth was another reason for wearing the slippers. Somewhat anemic from excessive dieting, Garbo often had cold hands and feet.

"Is the feets in?" she would ask when it came time to shoot.

If they were not, she would do the scene in slippers —incongruously topped by one of Adrian's dazzling creations. This habit allowed her creature comfort at the price of one of the enduring inaccuracies of the day. The Garbo feet are size 7-AA, and nicely shaped.

Garbo asked for Erich Von Stroheim to play with her in *As You Desire Me*. Von, as his friends called him, had earlier incurred Mayer's displeasure by making critical remarks about his own mother—mothers were sacred to Louis B. Mayer. He nonetheless bowed to Garbo's request, and Von Stroheim was hired. He rewarded her one day as she was putting on her shoes. "I don't think they're as ugly as people say," he remarked, to her vast amusement.

During the thirties Samuel Goldwyn became known as much for his garblings of the language, his "Goldwynisms," as for his films. Once this reputation was established, other people's Goldwyn-like comments were often attributed to him. It was Hungarian director Michael Curtiz, for example, who told a hapless messenger boy, "The next time I send a fool for something, I go myself." The remark attached itself to Goldwyn. Similarly, stories featuring aloofness and pursuit of privacy gravitated toward Garbo.

Contrary to the popular view there were no closed sets on the first Garbo films, though later she did demand them. The reason is technical. In the early films strong arc lights shone down on the acting area so that performers could not see beyond; the periphery was darkest black. Gradually equipment improved to the point where the entire set was evenly lit, almost as if by natural light. Now one could see past the periphery, out to where people were milling about and equipment being moved into position. This distracted Garbo, broke her concentration. She demanded that flats be erected around the set, with holes cut through, so that even the director would be outside her viewing range.

Conrad Nagel, Garbo's co-star in *The Mysterious Lady* and *The Kiss*, commented recently on the controversial closed sets: "She wasn't the only one. Nobody wants people to see them stumbling about in a scene, finding the way through. Everyone felt that way, wanted privacy, especially the directors. There was nothing unusual about Garbo's attitude."

Though other stars also demanded them, Garbo and closed sets became synonymous. They were cited as evidence of her temperament. It is true that Garbo was a sorceress when it came to detecting strangers on the set —although to no one's recollection was she ever impolite in her handling of the situation.

She was, however, firm and inflexible. She played no favorites, made no exceptions. Louis B. Mayer came to the set several times hoping to see his discovery in action. Once he brought along a board member he wished to impress. Garbo retired to her dressing room until her employer was gone.

Phil Scheuer, the film critic of the powerful Los Angeles *Times*, visited the set of *Romance* with Fritz Tidden, an aristocratic dwarf who was the personal representative of Clarence Brown.

"You'll have to leave now. She's coming," said Brown after they had talked. The two men headed for the far end of the set, a huge ballroom. Between them and Garbo were two hundred extras milling around a grand staircase. To the amazement of Scheuer and Tidden, she peered into the distance, fixing her eyes at the exact spot where they were in semi-hiding. Only after their departure could shooting begin.

Even an intimate friend like Salka Viertel was not allowed to visit her during shooting, and both William Daniels and Clarence Brown told friends that if Garbo had her way she'd make pictures without either of *them*.

While filming *Camille*, actor Rex O'Malley asked Garbo why she was so firm about the matter. "It destroys the illusion," she told him.

Various devices were used to sneak admiring strangers onto Garbo sets. They would be given scripts, and pencils to put behind their ears; each time she would sense an alien presence and quietly ask them to leave. The most elaborate deceit was practiced by Leif Erikson during the filming of *Conquest*. Erickson had sprained his back while riding a bicycle. This gave him a pretext for bringing a young actor friend to the set, masquerading as his doctor. The friend, Johnny Stearns, had studied at Peterborough with Maria Ouspenskaya, also in the cast and not privy to the maneuver.

"That doctor in the white suit will have to leave," Garbo said.

"That is not a doctor," said Ouspenskaya. "That is one of my best students."

Everyone including Garbo laughed—but "Doctor" Stearns was removed from the set of *Conquest*.

Garbo's insistence upon leaving work at precisely five in the afternoon was another trait widely discussed and analyzed in film circles. Constance Bennett left at four, and there were many others who left at five—but with Garbo it simply added to the legend. The Associated Press, learning one day that the actress had worked five minutes overtime, sent out a news release.

Actually, the AP missed other news beats. During the filming of *Mata Hari*, director George Fitzmaurice came to the male lead, Ramon Novarro, with a request. "We have a scene late in the day with some eighty to one hundred extras. If Miss Garbo would work one hour late we could finish the scene and dismiss all those extras. Would you mind asking her? You're such good friends."

Novarro invited Garbo to his dressing room and over a gin fizz asked her to stay late. She agreed on the extra hour. The scene was shot; the extras were dismissed. The next morning, however, the usually prompt actress evened the score by arriving two hours late.

Conrad Nagel's explanation of the Garbo working schedule and her "I tank I go home" remark, so often repeated in the thirties, was simple: "She concentrated more strongly on her acting than almost anyone I ever worked with, and so naturally at the end of the day she was tired and said 'I tank I go home.' She wasn't the only one. We all wanted to go home at the end of the day."

According to the legend Garbo could not be bothered either with fan mail or autographs. Author Mary Sale recalls that when she was a young player at Metro she appeared in a college musical which had a postoffice scene. She noticed that mail in the dummy postoffice was real; it was stamped, postmarked, addressed—and unopened. A closer look revealed that all the letters were addressed to Greta Garbo, care of Metro-Goldwyn-Mayer. During a break in the shooting, cast members ripped open the envelopes and found coins inside many of them—letters requesting photos or autographs or both had return postage enclosed.

These would not have bothered Garbo. But in the mail also came whispers of love, proposals of marriage, and a good deal of lurid pornography—graphic descriptions of what could be done to make her happy in bed. Photos giving proof of the sender's physical prowess sometimes accompanied the verbal erotica.

Many celebrities, male and female, receive this sort

of correspondence. Some rush to the mailbox each morning to see what new outrage is in store for them. Not Garbo. After *The Torrent*, her mail went unopened for months until the studio took over the handling of it.

In the early days Garbo had been willing to sign her name to a photo or a menu or a scrap of paper. At the time of *The Temptress*, she gave director Fred Niblo a photo with the inscription: "With a piece of my heart, Greta Garbo." This rare specimen is reproduced in this book. As her popularity grew and fans besieged her, the actress established a firm policy. She gave her autograph to no one, not even her co-stars.

As was the case with other aspects of the Garbo mystique, her refusal made the prize more sought after. During the filming of *Camille* Garbo became ill. A number of players in the cast sent flowers, knowing that politeness dictated a return card. In each case a card duly arrived. On it was one word: "Thanks."

Even today Garbo is reluctant with her signature, and Garbo letters signed with the name are suspect. She does correspond but almost invariably prints her message.

Garbo made no exceptions to her no-autograph policy. Once, during the war, host Sherman Billingsley came to her table at the Stork Club in New York. Behind him was a young soldier, an amputee in a wheelchair.

"Miss Garbo," said Billingsley, "I know you will get the greatest pleasure from the request I am going to make. Will you autograph the menu of this boy?"

"I never gif my autograph," said Garbo.

The soldier was wheeled away.

Garbo's position on such matters as closed sets and autographs must be viewed in the context of her unprecedented status as a superstar. In the thirties, touching —or even glimpsing—Greta Garbo became a national neurosis. "Forget Yellowstone and Coney Island and the Grand Canyon," wrote Leonard Hall in 1931. "The sands of Hollywood are white with the bleaching bones of ferocious flappers who perished of starvation while waiting for Garbo to emerge from her Santa Monica deadfall and go down to the store for a pint of milk. Thousands have drowned while lurking behind shrubbery in the hope of seeing her come out for a walk in the rain."

In an article for *Photoplay* Hall defined his subject: "She could ride around Hollywood on a howling hyena and leading a stuffed duck and it would be all right with the Garbomaniacs. Garbo gets away with personal idiosyncrasy that would send other stars' fans shrieking away in droves."

His own encomium followed: "It is probable that in the whole history of the world no artist ever grew to such great glory on utter heedlessness of what anybody thinks, says, or writes. . . . She is the one great queen of the screen who not only has never courted public favor but has actually fought to a standstill all attempts to haul her into the limelight. Whether it is a trick or the nature of the lady, it is absolutely perfect. I smile skeptically at the odd spectacle of Greta Garbo and yet I genuflect in admiration. As the race of queens dies out and is replaced by erring, faulty, frail men and women, she alone remains—the greatest and loneliest of a mighty line."

Without doubt, Garbo paid a high price for adula-

tion bordering on the psychotic. Among her worshippers, women no less than men were guilty of paying
her excessive tribute. When Garbo gave up the Miramar
in 1932 and moved into the Beverly Hills Hotel, she
never appeared for dinner or drinks. Fashionable society
figures and quaint kooks sat patiently in the lobby hoping to catch a glimpse of her. One young idolator stalked
the lobby until she heard scraps of conversation indicat-
ing Garbo's car was being brought forth. Unobtrusively,
Garbo entered her shopworn Packard. The chauffeur
was easing the car out of the driveway when the star-
struck fan threw herself in front of the automobile.
Garbo was alarmed, but no harm was done. Several years
later, the same girl appeared at her door. Garbo turned
her away.

The Garbomaniacs in wait at every corner unques-
tionably frightened the star. She moved into a modest
rambling home of her own, her first house in America,
at 1027 Chevy Chase in Beverly Hills. Fan magazines
immediately published the address. At midnight there
were wolf cries—the Shriners were in town. The children next door sold tickets for treetop views of Garbo
sunning herself by the pool. Her discarded cigarette
butts brought premium prices.

A treasured story of the period said that one night
Garbo became so alarmed by people ringing her bell
that she rushed outside, climbed a tree, and shouted "Not
in" from her perch whenever the buzzer sounded.

Friends who called were sometimes amused by a
servant's message: "Miss Garbo says to say she is not in."

After her initial successes in Hollywood, Garbo took
a vacation trip to her native Sweden. When she tried to

make her departure without fanfare, the press unleashed a barrage of criticism reviewing her multiple sins. "Crowned heads, millionaires, famous writers visiting Hollywood have expressed desires to meet Garbo. She has refused. Who is she, we ask, to presume to behave like that?" asked a film trade journal. "She refused to meet Lady Mountbatten when she visited the studios, refused to meet a royal personage from her own country, refused to have tea with Marlene Dietrich. And to nice, spontaneous Joan Crawford whose dressing room for many years was next to hers in Metro's star corridor, she has in all that time addressed scarcely a dozen words. . . . Greta Garbo has left the country without saying goodbye, without even suggesting that she was sorry to go. Who is she that she can permit herself such behavior, the world's greatest actress? Well, and what if she is? Sarah Bernhardt was and so was Eleanor Duse, but neither turned her back on the press and public."

In Sweden, Garbomaniacs clawed to get at their idol, even broke the windows of a limousine in which she was riding. The trip turned into a flight from crowds.

A visit to New York provoked chases and near riots. Garbomaniacs jammed the lobby of the Hotel St. Moritz, hoping to see or touch their idol. When she went shopping on Fifth Avenue, the crowd ripped off her coat buttons and pulled at her gloves, sending her running back to her hotel. When she wanted to walk in Central Park, an entire battalion of taxis followed her, reporters and photographers in hot pursuit. At the Casino in the Park she threw a bill at her driver and got out. The other cabs stopped. Garbo ran. Reporters ran. Photographers ran. Finally, she turned to face the pack.

"I feel sorry for you. You haf such a tough job," she said, then hopped into another cab.

During evening hours a telescope in Central Park, where a dime brought a view of the constellations, was trained on the St. Moritz. In one room a Garbo double walked back and forth. The charge for the waiting line of suckers was a quarter.

Garbo doubles were not all unauthorized. The star's reluctance to have the clothes torn from her back by berserk souvenir hunters gave a brief moment in the sun to her stand-in, Geraldine De Vorak. A look-alike in face and figure, Geraldine was described by one wit as having "everything that Garbo has except whatever it is that Garbo has."

Once Garbo was a star, it was De Vorak who sat long hours for costume fittings and stood in the glare of the lights while scenes were being set up. It was she also who sometimes wore Garbo's gowns to smart restaurants and nightclubs, enjoying the spotlight which Garbo shunned.

Other stars flaunted their celebrity. Pola Negri walked down the street with a pet cheetah on a leash. Henry Wilcoxon, DeMille's handsome star, would emerge from his apartment at the Garden of Allah with one falcon perched on his wrist and another on his shoulder. Clara Bow zipped down Sunset Boulevard in a Kissel Kar with six red chow dogs surrounding her. Lilyan Tashman served her cat high tea in the afternoon. Everyone in this gaudy era was doing his thing. Garbo's was to escape the public eye, and hers turned out to be the most effective of all the gambits in vogue.

It certainly helped preserve a romantic distance between the star and her American moviegoing audience, to whom she seemed enigmatic, even phantasmic. To the co-workers with whom she made twenty-four Holly-wood films, Garbo was far more real. The impressions they formed of her were varied and sometimes contra-dictory, but overall a portrait emerges of a woman complex and changeable, with moods and attributes far more characteristic of a mortal than of an unapproach-able goddess.

WILLIAM DANIELS

Daniels, the man behind the cameras for eighteen of Garbo's Hollywood films, came to Metro in his twenties after six years as cameraman for Erich von Stroheim at Universal.

"I'm a salesman, and part of my job is selling portraits of beautiful women," Louis B. Mayer told him. "It's up to you to give me those portraits."

Daniels studied Garbo's face and body with great care. He saw immediately that she was least attractive in repose, best in closeups or long shots, indifferent in the intermediate range. She was better seated or lying down than standing—Daniels later shot some of her best love scenes, in *Flesh and the Devil* and *Queen Christina*, with Garbo reclining. (The position also favored her leading men, who were often shorter than she.)

While it is generally assumed that shooting a Garbo picture was a solemn affair, the mood on set was often lighthearted. The youthful crew developed various run-ning gags. One electrician would let out a piercing yell everytime he approached Daniels, pretending to be hurt by him. Garbo enjoyed the clowning, laughing when the electrician let out the familiar shriek while a full fifty feet away from Daniels.

On the last day of each film, Garbo would shyly bring gifts, most of which she bought at an expensive downtown import store. Daniels still prizes beautiful cloisonné pieces, as well as a solid gold cigarette case, a silver bowl, and a richly embroidered Chinese tapestry.

"No one felt she was untouchable," he says. "She was often quite gay, and so were we all."

Daniels recalls a scene in *Romance* in which an organ-grinder's monkey comes to Garbo's window and hands her a tin cup containing a message from her lover. As she reached for the cup, the monkey bit her. She was neither flustered nor angry. She lifted the monkey's skirt, spanked him lightly, and said "Stop that." The impromptu episode was retained in the picture.

"Garbo was invariably understanding," says Daniels. "That's what was in those eyes. In my early years I was strongly drawn to my grandmother, who seemed to have the most beautiful feeling for people and life. It amazed me to find that same feeling in Garbo, a very young woman.

"The saddest thing in my career is that I was never able to photograph her in color. I begged the studio. I felt I had to get those incredible blue eyes in color, but they said no. The process at the time was cumbersome and expensive, and the pictures were already making money. I still feel sad about it."

CLARENCE BULL

While Garbo withdrew almost completely from the publicity arena, she continued throughout her career to comply with one of its demands. At the end of each picture she would allow Clarence Bull, who ran the still photographic laboratory, to take publicity portraits and make poster stills of the familiar parts of the film. From 1925 to 1940 Garbo came in an average of twice a year, usually for two days of work. Unlike many other stars, she was invariably fifteen minutes early and perfectly cooperative as Bull made up to three hundred shots, a total over the years of more than seven thousand. Throughout their long relationship he always remained "Mr. Bull" and she "Miss Garbo."

"I think she appreciated the way I worked—quietly," says Bull. "I never said, 'Still!' or 'Hold it!'—words which often affect people like an electric shock. I would give her the general pose. She would look out of the corner of her eye to see if her interpretation was registering on me, and if so, she would hold it. I might make a gesture, and then she would repeat it, showing me how it was really done. We hardly spoke. Her eyes would roam and as she assumed a pose she could tell by looking at me whether it was what I wanted or not. She always knew.

"After the sessions, Garbo would come in and look at proofs. By that time I would have checked the negatives and culled out a few, not many, because it was almost impossible to take a bad picture of Garbo. She always amazed me, though.

" 'We took more than that,' she would say.

" 'Some of them were not too good.'

" 'Did I do something wrong?'

" 'No, I did. The lighting didn't please me.'

"How she could ask about those few discarded proofs when we took three hundred in all mystified me.

"Her memory was phenomenal, anyway. During one session I had a new assistant who was excited to be working around Garbo. He was moving a baby spotlight when it fell and hit her on the shoulder.

" 'I'll sit still,' she said. 'You don't have to knock me out.'

"Years later she saw the same man, not in my gallery but elsewhere, and recognized him immediately. " 'Do you still throw spotlights at people?' she asked.

"There are so many stories like that about Garbo. One electrician's wife was in the hospital when a call came that she was about to give birth. The electrician hurried down a ladder where he was working, missed a few steps, and bruised himself. Garbo saw the incident and remembered it years later when she saw the man again. 'Your little girl must be about five years old now,' she said, hitting the figure exactly.

"She had a nice sense of humor, too. Everyone knows about those famous long eyelashes. I had photographed them a thousand times but one day I was looking at them rather closely. Garbo asked if something was wrong.

" 'No,' I said, teasing her, 'I was just wondering if they're your lashes.'

" 'Pull 'em,' she said.

"After Garbo came onto the scene all the girls

started wearing false eyelashes. Hers were real, of course.

"I had a problem keeping people from stealing Garbo stills. I mean important people. Hedda Hopper admitted to me that she stole more Garbo prints than anyone, including some from the archives at the Academy of Motion Picture Arts and Sciences.

"Everyone wanted her autograph on a photo. One day George Cukor came in while Garbo was there and asked her to sign one for him. She did, but she made him promise not to use it for publication. Well, not long after, it found its way into a magazine and Cukor called me. He was furious. What happened was that someone had interviewed Cukor in his office. When Cukor stepped out for a moment the reporter used a hidden pocket camera to snap the autographed Garbo photo, and printed it.

"It was like that in those days."

KARL FREUND

"I met Garbo when she was with Stiller in Berlin. In Hollywood I was cameraman on *Conquest*, and on part of *Camille*.

" 'G.G., what do you do when you go home?' I asked her one day.

" 'I rest a bit, the maid brings me dinner, then I study the next day's script and go to bed. I've been in my new house for three months and would you believe it, I've never seen the living room. I eat, study, and sleep.'

" 'And what else do you do?'

" 'I sometimes play checkers, with myself.'

" 'And what do you do about sex?'

" 'Once in a while I go out, when I meet a man I like who enjoys me. When he arrives I peek out at him to see what he's wearing and then I dress accordingly. Many of the men who ask me out go crazy about my Swedish maid, who is very pretty. They pat her on the cheek and flirt with her, but for me, at the end of the evening they say, 'Thank you, Miss Garbo,' and they tell me how wonderful it was but not one ever says, 'Let's go to bed.'

" 'That's the price you pay for being famous,' I said."

RAMON NOVARRO *

"I liked Garbo very much although it seems to me she was impersonal. I don't think she was ever in love with anyone. Someone must have frightened her at the beginning. They say Stiller hit her.

"Clarence Brown said no one got on so well so fast with her as I did. Perhaps it was because I was Mexican and she was Swedish, two foreigners. We went out sometimes, but not often. We were all working so hard. At the end of the day we were tired.

"I often wondered how Garbo knew when it was just exactly five o'clock, her quitting time. Then one day I learned. Alma, her colored maid, would raise up

---

* Editor's note: The author's interview with Mr. Novarro was the last granted by the actor before his murder in late 1968.

the makeup-box mirror as a signal. When Garbo saw it, she started taking the pins out of her hair without losing another moment.

"During the filming of *Mata Hari*, Garbo always wanted to rehearse the love scenes with me in private. She needed to be able to concentrate. She had to convince herself before she could convince anyone else.

"Did Garbo invent herself? Did publicity invent her? It was meant to be. Garbo was mysterious without trying."

FREDRIC MARCH

"As the saying went at the time, co-starring with Garbo hardly constituted an introduction. Earlier, in the days when she saw a lot of Jack Gilbert, we'd play tennis there and Garbo was just another vital, healthy, strong Swedish girl. But then something happened and she retreated.

"During the making of *Anna Karenina* she was very friendly, not always reserved. We would bounce a medicine ball back and forth during breaks, and one day she stripped to the waist to take the sun. Then she caught herself and asked if it embarrassed me. It did not.

"She had a fine sense of humor. I told her one day how wonderful she had been with the boy in the silent version of *Anna Karenina*, letting him really take over their scenes together. I suggested maybe she should adopt a child.

" 'A little late in the picture for you to make such a proposition to me,' she said.

"Actually I was not overwhelmed by Garbo's beauty. I think at the time women were more attracted to her than men."

FREDDIE BARTHOLOMEW

"The only thing I remember about Garbo in *Anna Karenina* is that she was very charming and sweet. I vaguely recall being told that she was a very special lady who demanded total privacy. I was warned of that and was pleasantly surprised when she turned out to be very nice. I did have one terrible disappointment because I liked her and wanted a picture of her but when I asked she said, 'No, I do not give pictures.' This is my friend, I thought, and was sad."

ROBERT TAYLOR

"I was scared to death at the thought of appearing with Garbo in *Camille*. Needlessly. She was a fantastic human being. She loved acting and the people she worked with and there was never any problem at all. There were few retakes because of Garbo but many retakes on the picture because MGM wanted to make each scene perfect. We shot the death scene three separate times, not because there was anything wrong with it but just to keep improving it.

"I don't think Garbo was a Method actress, but she certainly knew what it was all about. One of the great secrets of acting, of course, is to think. I've never learned it, but Garbo knew. She thought with her eyes, photo-graphically. The muscles in her face would not move, and yet her eyes would express exactly what was needed. Working with her was perhaps my greatest acting lesson, though I probably didn't learn enough from it.

"Ten years ago I saw Garbo again for the first time since making the picture. She was dining in the MGM commissary and my companion suggested I go over and say hello. I would no more go over to Garbo than I would drop dead in the commissary. I respect her feeling for privacy too much.

"If she ever makes another picture, I want to buy the first ticket."

REX O'MALLEY

"I was never really interested in films, nor was I a fan of Garbo's. But when I was cast in *Camille* and found myself in an early scene next to her in an opera box, I came close to swooning over her beautiful honey-colored hair and shoulders.

"I liked her sense of humor. Once when we were dancing in a scene she started giving way, and over she went. I fell, too, as gently as possible, right on top of her. She burst into laughter. 'It's my little feet,' she said.

"Another day, when the death scene was being filmed, the lighting wasn't exactly what they wanted and there were retakes. After three times, as she lay there dying in bed, Garbo suddenly became hysterical with laughter. She wouldn't explain."

LEIF ERICKSON

"Paramount loaned me to Metro to make *Conquest*, in which I played Garbo's brother. In one scene, on a staircase, I was supposed to take hold of Garbo. When I did, her gown got caught on a button of my uniform and ripped. There was Garbo in the altogether. Well, I fell back and looked at her in amazement. Instead of getting angry, she smiled. 'I thought that would inspire you,' she said.

"Garbo is the hippie of the world, surveying the scene, never partaking of it, not even active enough to pass judgment. She becomes a mirror, and others finally see themselves in her. It reminds me of soldiers in a riot. If they don't move against the crowd, if they just stand still, the crowd finally quiets and sees itself. Garbo's quiet makes people see themselves in her, and finally they want to become like her."

ROBERT STERLING

"I liked her tremendously. When George Cukor introduced me on the set of *Two-Faced Woman*, she was seated. She looked up at me with that incredible face and offered her hand.

"You are so rosy," she said.

"She invited me to lunch several times in her dressing room. We talked and became friends. It was a gay set, on *Two-Faced Woman*, no one felt we were making anything but a fine picture. There was a lot of clowning on the set.

" 'Everybody is always laughing and no one tells me anything funny,' she said to me one day.

" 'Well you're always hiding, for godssake,' I told her, and that made her laugh.

"Garbo was truly sensitive. For some reason, Constance Bennett didn't like me. On one occasion we were all seated at a table rehearsing for a master scene— Roland Young, Melvyn Douglas, Ruth Gordon, Garbo, and Bennett. 'I'm serving tea in my dressing room, Bennett said during a break. She thereupon invited each one, conspicuously omitting me. Garbo refused her invitation and invited me to tea in *her* dressing room.

"I recently saw Garbo in New York, walking in the street. I debated saying hello but decided against it. I respected her wish for privacy."

CLARENCE BROWN

"If Garbo had had the ambition to really study English and to study the techniques of acting, she could have been another Sarah Bernhardt. Those eyes, for one thing. I've seen her change from love to hate and never alter her facial expression. I would be somewhat unhappy and take the scene again. The expression still would not change. Still unhappy, I would go ahead and say, 'Print it.' And when I looked at the print, there it was. The eyes told it all. Her face wouldn't change but on the screen would be that transition from love to hate.

"Garbo didn't die in every film, but in general she

could die or be killed at the end and one could get away with it. It couldn't be done with Shearer or other heroines, the public wouldn't stand for it.

"She had a droll sense of humor and she could be clever. While working with her in *Anna Karenina*, Fredric March showed signs of wanting to get romantic. Before each love scene Garbo put a small piece of garlic in her mouth. It worked.

"There's a story about her that I think very few people know. I worked for Louis B. Mayer for twenty-five years, and in the last five or six years of his life we were very close. He once told me about the days after *Two-Faced Woman*, Garbo's last picture, a dismal flop. Mayer knew that the European market was gone, where Garbo was so strong. And things looked shaky in the American market, too. But Garbo's contract still had some time to run. Mayer called her in to explain the market situation. He told her they did not want to make another picture but that they would pay her as provided by her contract. With that he handed her a check for two hundred thousand dollars.

" 'No, Mr. Mayer, I did not earn it,' said Garbo very simply, and handed it back.

GEORGE CUKOR

"She's a very original kind of actress. The director was wise to give her leeway. She knew an enormous amount about what the camera could do. She was very subtle, able with a slight gesture to be enormously suggestive. In her erotic scenes in *Camille*, to give an example, she never touches but kisses her lover all over the face. Often she is the aggressor in lovemaking, reaching first. Very original.

"Yes, I still see her. She was here to dinner the other night. She came with Gayelord Hauser. Mae West was there—Garbo wanted to see the spiked shoes which make Mae taller. And Mae saw that Garbo's feet are not large after all. Garbo was dressed very simply. She sat in front of Mae, who was swathed in a gown. They all talked about their health regimes. They're all health nuts."

MARGARET BOOTH

"I was one of the few women ever allowed on a Garbo set. I was the film editor on *Mysterious Lady*, *Susan Lenox*, and *Camille*. In the early days, before she had lost Stiller and her sister, Garbo was quite gay. I think, though, that she found Americans cold, that they did not give her much affection.

"One day I was at Bullock's inspecting some yard goods, and there at my side was Garbo. She was wearing her large floppy hat and I thought she probably didn't want to be recognized, so I said nothing. The next day at the studio she came over to me and said, 'Margaret, why didn't you speak to me yesterday?'

"Where did it all begin? People think Garbo wants to be alone and so they let her alone, and she thinks they don't want to speak to her and lets *them* alone. And so, there's the legend of being aloof."

BILLY WILDER

"Her face is amazing. It has such uniqueness, such luminosity that it touches everyone. You read into it what you like.

"In her acting Garbo has a sense of the mood, of the texture, of the instinct, without perhaps being very bright. Others can act their ass to shreds and nothing happens. But Garbo has a sixth sense, like Marilyn Monroe had, a sense for what is appropriate.

"It may be the goddamnedest put-on of all time, yet Garbo is the quintessence of what a star should be. Today's actresses tell us how they bring up their children and give us their recipe for scrambled eggs, but Garbo stumbled on a much more compelling idea. She said and did nothing and let the world write her story. She was as incongruous in Hollywood as Sibelius would have been if he had come to write incidental music for Warner Brothers films." *

WALTER REISCH

"I don't think many people have seen Garbo cry, but I did, the year that *Ninotchka* was released and all the papers were full of huge ads saying, 'Garbo laughs.'

* Author's Note: Wilder gives his aging actress in *Sunset Boulevard* the line, "In those days we had faces." She is referring to silent pictures and mentions a number of names, including Garbo's. After seeing the film Garbo, evidently dismayed by the past tense, told a friend, "I thought Billy Wilder was a friend of mine."

"It was in June of 1940. Mussolini had just announced that Italy would enter the war and Roosevelt was going to make a speech at the University of Virginia. I was in producer Gottfried Reinhardt's office listening to the radio. Salka Viertel was there, too, composers Arthur Goodman and Dr. Bronislav Kaper, and also John McLain. We were all surprised when Garbo appeared at the door. She was wearing blue slacks and a sweater, one of her enormous straw hats, sandals, no makeup. She had heard the radio and asked if she could come in. She sat and when Roosevelt started talking she listened very intently.

" 'The government of Italy has now chosen to preserve what it terms its freedom of action,' he said. 'On this tenth day of June 1940 the hand that held the dagger has stuck it into the back of its neighbor . . .'

"FDR's voice so moved Garbo that she dissolved into tears. We were all looking at her to see her reaction, but she didn't seem to care. 'Does anyone have a Kleenex?' she asked.

"MGM's Eddie Mannix had told Ernst Lubitsch he could direct *Ninotchka* if he could persuade Garbo to star in it. She wouldn't go to Lubitsch's house, nor he to hers, so Salka Viertel arranged for them to meet at the Villa Nova. Garbo arrived, said she was on a diet and would just listen as he discussed the film. Poor Lubitsch had ordered an immense meal—the antipasto, a dozen special dishes, and the chianti, and the frutti, and the cheeses were already on the table.

" 'I never touch lunch,' Garbo said.

" 'All right,' said Lubitsch. 'I will eat and you listen.' He started telling Garbo the story. He got more excited with each line, and forgot the food. An hour later, when he had finished talking, he looked at the table—it was cleaned out. Garbo had been so carried away by his enthusiasm that she had forgotten her diet and put away the whole meal.

"Because we had worked on *Ninotchka*, which was a success, Billy Wilder and I later tried to get Garbo interested in a comeback idea. It was 1948 or so and we arranged to meet at Billy's house. First he was to tell a story to try and get her interested, then I was to tell one.

"Billy started with the *Inconnue de la Seine*, the famous death mask in the Louvre, and developed the story of an unknown girl, drowned, reconstructing her life as the wife of a banker.

" 'I do not want to play the wife of a banker,' Garbo said.

"Billy's wife offered refreshments.

" 'I will haf a nikolaijecek,' said Garbo, referring to a drink made by slipping a slice of lemon on the tongue, dissolving sugar on that same spot, and washing it down with a light brandy.

"Then I took my turn, telling the story of Elizabeth of Austria, the most beautiful woman of the nineteenth century, an empress whose one temptation as a woman was to run away, abdicate, and be herself.

" 'Another nikolaijecek,' said Garbo.

" 'But what about the story?'

" 'I haf played Queen Christina already and I do not want to play another empress,' she said.

"I drove Garbo home, and on the way tried one more approach.

" 'Greta, if you ever wanted to make a comeback,

give us one hint of what you would like to do. Do you want to play an actress, a spy, a coquette, a scientist?'

" 'A clown. A male clown.'

" 'The most desired woman on earth wants to play a clown? Who will buy that?'

" 'Under the makeup and the silk pants, the clown is a woman. And all the admiring girls in the audience who write him letters are wondering why he does not respond. They cannot understand.'

" 'It will never do,' I said.

"We never got any further."

RALPH WHEELRIGHT

"We in publicity had little contact with her. Her degree of cooperation was nonexistent, but we would find items and any item you wrote was immediately printed. Earl Wilson went up in an elevator with her and that became a story.

"The department came to know what she considered an invasion of privacy. At the beginning she did the best she could to cooperate but she had nothing to say to the creatures who wanted to know the secrets of her love life and other things she felt her private domain. Just before *A Single Standard*, we were over in Catalina on location when a reporter kept jumping out at her from behind doors and bushes. Once, he accosted her and all she said was 'Damn!' It became known as the famous one-word interview."

BENNY THAU

"Of course when she worked for us at the studio I saw her. My wife and I saw her recently out here, but I could not say anything to you about her. I would never say anything about this woman without permission."

SIDNEY GUILAROFF

"The Garbo look? She was born with it. No one had to do much about it. All the lines in her face went up, where with most people they come down. She was unique.

"Yes, I saw Garbo when she was out here this spring but I'm not going to talk about her."

ROBERT MONTGOMERY

"I'm not interested in discussing Garbo."

Garbo told the world she did nothing but work, eat, and sleep, that she hated dancing and parties, and the world believed her. But the fact is that she went to a great many parties, and she sometimes danced, and usually drank vodka, and was quite gay.

For a time there were the Jack Gilbert soirees. She also partied at the Irving Thalbergs, at Pola Negri's, at William Randolph Hearst's famous twin-peaked castle up the coast, San Simeon. She went to San Francisco for gatherings at the home of Robert Watt Miller, chairman of the board of Pacific Lighting Corporation. There, if she knew all the other guests, she would do pointed, funny imitations of other Hollywood stars; if there were strangers present, she tended to be silent. Garbo attended one party at Ouida and Basil Rathbone's without anyone there knowing until the next day that she had been present. Photos showed that the slim masked youth costumed as Prince Hamlet was Garbo.

The number of gatherings attended by Garbo was in fact astonishing. It is hard to find anyone who was in Hollywood during the thirties who doesn't have a story to tell about Garbo at a large party, or an intimate dinner, or a spontaneous drop-in affair. Everyone invited her—perhaps because she made no effort to meet anyone, because she said she never went out.

Even among other prominent stars, she was an object of intense interest and curiosity. On one occasion Irene Dunne, working at the time on an adjacent set, sat in her car and waited for Garbo to appear, as eager as the most star-struck fan.

Tallulah Bankhead, who had her own band of worshippers, was wildly anxious to meet Garbo. Among her friends were Berthold and Salka Viertel. Tallulah knew how protective Salka was of her close relationship with Garbo, and she and her friends consequently swore to keep the Garbo name off their tongues, referring to her always as "that person." The game went further. If anyone did mention Garbo, he had to give each of the others in the group a dollar. One evening, as Tallulah, actor Allen Vincent, and others were headed for the Viertel home, everyone was unusually silent.

"Well, you might think we were going to see Garbo," said Tallulah.

She had to pay up. To everyone's amazement and delight, Garbo was there when they arrived. Salka could never understand why her guests all laughed when Garbo entered the room.

Tallulah and Garbo got on famously, and Garbo later came to dinner parties given by Tallulah. On one occasion, Garbo and several others were already at the house when Ethel Barrymore joined them.

"Miss Barrymore, Miss Garbo," said hostess Tallulah. Barrymore was at her most imperial, but even she appeared startled by Garbo's beauty. She recovered her aplomb and held out her hand; Garbo took it, and when Barrymore sat down in a chair and set up court, Garbo was at her feet. The evening went extremely well.

"Forget all the bilge about Garbo," Tallulah wrote in her autobiography. "She's excessively shy. When at ease with people who do not look upon her as something begat by the Sphinx and Frigga, Norse goddess of the sky, she can be as much fun as the next gal."

Always aware of the impact she made, Garbo was hard to pin down when it came to invitations. She knew she was expected to be on display, when she wanted spontaneity. As a result she tended to withhold acceptances until the last minute, and took to casually dropping in on friends.

One day Gayelord Hauser brought her unannounced

to see King Kennedy. King introduced them to his mother, a socially prominent dowager who knew little about the film world.

"What do you do, little girl?" she asked.

Garbo loved it.

The beach house of Anita Loos was a film colony social center in the thirties. It was on the Santa Monica Riviera, a handsome strand where Louis B. Mayer, the Thalbergs, William Randolph Hearst, Bebe Daniels and Ben Lyon, and others maintained elaborate residences. Anita's young niece, Mary Sale, was there one day at a moment of great excitement. Garbo had arrived—uninvited—with Leopold Stokowski. She was wearing wool knickers fastened below the knees, golf socks, a straw hat like a Mexican peanut vendor, no makeup, her hair loose.

"What do you do?" she asked Mary.

"I'm an archaeologist but I think I really want to be an actress."

"You should be. You're very pretty."

"Thank you, but I'm afraid I'm too tall."

"No, you are not too tall." She placed a book on her head, and made Mary stand back to back with her, proving that they were the same height.

On certain rare occasions, Garbo's habit of dropping in was not appreciated. The widow of a prominent director who lived down the road from Garbo in Santa Monica invited Allen Vincent and Tallulah Bankhead for dinner one day. As they moved into the living room for coffee, the doorbell rang.

"Why, there's Garbo," said Tallulah.

"She wasn't asked," said the hostess.

The drop-in was one ploy the actress used to help her escape a Garbo-obsessed society; taking pseudonyms was another. Garbo has used many—Harriet Brown, Gussie Berger, Mary Holmquist, Jean Clark, Karin Lund, Miss Swanson, Emily Clark, Jane Emerson, Alice Smith, and even a male sobriquet, Karl Lund. The overall favorite has been Harriet Brown.

When the popular English playwright and performer Ivor Novello came to Hollywood in the thirties, George Cukor asked him whether there were any special treat he might arrange for him.

"I have only one desire—to meet Garbo," said Novello.

"Done," said Cukor. "But I must tell you that at the moment she does not want to be known as Garbo. You must live with the fiction that she is Harriet Brown."

Novello followed the instruction. He and "Miss Brown" got on beautifully, comparing notes on the many acquaintances they had in common. They met a second and third time at Cukor's. In the warmth of their developing friendship Novello had an inspiration.

"Miss Brown," he said, "now that we know each other so well—do you think I might call you Harriet?"

Withdrawing from public functions, dropping in, using pseudonyms are often cited as proof of Garbo's shyness. They are better seen as illustrating her sense of values. Crowds and obvious celebrity seekers led her not to shun human company but to consciously seek out the genuine in human relationships.

Even as a child she placed a high premium on sincerity, on candor. She was willing to offer much to her friends but she also exacted certain demands. Biogra-

pher Fritiof Billquist has quoted a letter Garbo wrote
at fourteen to a schoolmate:

"If you and I are to continue friends, you must
keep away from my girl friends, as I did from yours . . .
Eva, I am arrogant and impatient by nature. . . . If this
letter offends you, then you don't need to write to me
again, but if it doesn't and you will promise to behave
as a friend, then I shall be glad to hear from you again
soon."

In Hollywood Garbo was no less firm. "The minute
they exploit her in the public prints, as they invariably
do, she banishes them from the court of Garbo," wrote
one observer. "If you're Garbo's friend and would remain so you've got to take the oath of silence."

In mid-career costumer Gilbert Adrian agreed to
answer twenty questions about Garbo. He knew he was
risking the loss of her friendship, he said, but there were
so many misquotes about her circulating that he felt
compelled to correct them.

"She is decidedly a woman apart, because she is actually so simple and has not one ounce of affectation," he
said at one point. "She is at no moment the actress and
never gives me the illusion of being one until she is
on the set before the lights, actually in the part. The
minute she leaves the set she's a very little girl, completely out of her atmosphere because she so consistently
lives her life the way she wants to regardless of critics
or the suggestions of her friends. She cannot help but
be different.

"Sometimes I think because she lives so remotely she
appears not to need friendship as much as most people
do. I think, however, that she can be a great friend—

provided the friend can adjust himself or herself to Garbo's viewpoint on life."

In the late twenties Stiller and Gilbert had been the dominant figures in Garbo's life. In the thirties, those closest to her were Salka Viertel, Mercedes d'Acosta, Rouben Mamoulian, Gayelord Hauser, and Leopold Stokowski.

Salka Viertel and her husband Berthold had distinguished themselves in Europe before coming to Hollywood in the twenties. Berthold won acclaim for his direction of *Adventures of a Ten-Mark Note* and other films; Polish-born Salka had forged a career on the German stage, first with Max Reinhardt and later with her own company.

In Hollywood she played the Marie Dressler role in the German version of *Anna Christie,* but she soon turned to writing screenplays. It was Salka who suggested that Garbo make a film version of the life of Sweden's Queen Christina. With H. M. Harwood she wrote the scenario, which told the story of a strong monarch, a woman who affects masculine dress and stubbornly refuses to marry. Salka also worked on the screenplay for Garbo's next film, an adaptation of Somerset Maugham's *The Painted Veil,* and *Anna Karenina,* which Garbo had already made in the silent version called *Love.* Her other Garbo screenwriting credits were *Conquest* and *Two-Faced Woman.*

Garbo tends to be attracted to strong women, particularly when they are intellectual and artistic as well. Salka Viertel was all of these—a handsome, bright, witty, worldly woman, described by one friend as predatory in her pursuit of life. She and Garbo were instantly drawn to one another, talking easily about their European backgrounds and the contrast with Hollywood, and about life, that all-encompassing four-letter word. Salka stimulated Garbo's mind and her aesthetic sense, amused her with trenchant comments on her contemporaries. "I wish I could be like you," Garbo told her one day. "If I had your vitality and temperament, I'd be world famous."

Garbo began to depend on Salka, who cultivated this aspect of their relationship. She became her career advisor, recommending story ideas and developing them. So close were the two that studio executives, when they found Garbo incommunicado, would use Salka as an intermediary.

The two women's social life continued apace, for Salka was a beacon for the European colony in Hollywood. The relationship between the much older Salka and Garbo continued throughout the thirties, until the end of Garbo's film career. Distance then separated the two, as Garbo wandered. Friends report that Salka's earlier ardor for Garbo cooled, for undisclosed reasons, but in recent years the friendship has been renewed.

"I'm going to Hollywood to meet Garbo," Mercedes D'Acosta is reported to have told friends in Paris in the late twenties. At the time it was not an easy thing to do, but Mercedes, the daughter of a proud and eccentric Spanish family, brought off the coup. She had grown up among an international elite of talented figures. Short, stylish, and deep-voiced, she was a poet and playwright, a nonconformist in many ways, including dress and makeup—in one period she rouged her earlobes and sported a tricornered Princess Eugenie hat.

Mercedes was proud of her accomplishments and of the circles she frequented. On one occasion she told of losing someone dear to her and of how kind her friends, especially those from the theatre, had been to her in her bereavement. She then reeled off a list that included Noel Coward, Harold Ross, Alexander Woollcott, Alfred Lunt, Lynn Fontanne, Clifton Webb, Katherine Cornell, "and countless others."

In Hollywood she turned to screenwriting. She met Garbo at Salka Viertel's house on Mabery Road. In her autobiography, *Here Lies the Heart,* she describes the encounter: "As we shook hands and she smiled at me I felt that I had known her all my life; in fact, in many previous incarnations."

A certain mysticism characterized both Garbo and Mercedes. Mercedes was a faddist—a vegetarian, a student of Oriental philosophies, full of odd ideas about the arts. Garbo has always liked faddists. She became a willing disciples of Mercedes' energetic exploration of life. The two owned houses near one another and visited back and forth regularly. They vacationed together, both in America and abroad.

Like Salka Viertel, Mercedes suggested screen roles for Garbo, and on similar themes. She developed one idea which called for Garbo to dress as a boy. Irving Thalberg turned it down as commercially unsound. She also approached the studio with story ideas based on St. Francis, Teresa of Avila, and Joan of Arc, devoting several months to the Joan concept before Garbo turned it down. Garbo herself said she wanted to play Dorian Gray, but no one took her up on that.

"She is reticent but the stories about her shyness are incorrect—she is never *shy*," wrote Mercedes. "She is emotional and fears showing it. When she is among people she can be gay and full of fun but alone she tends to become serious and melancholic. I understand this because Spaniards are like that. . . .

"Garbo can more thoroughly evoke an emotion of pity and defense than anyone I have ever known, at least in me. Though there may be nothing particular to defend her against, I want to protect her, to take her part. This may be because there is a strange sadness in her underlying everything she does. . . . This is the hold I believe she has on the public.

"People have sometimes said that she has little talent for friendship. Her problem is that her standards of friendship are so high few people can meet them."

When she started to write about Garbo, Mercedes expressed her apprehensions. She knew her friend hated being discussed, she said, and that the book would cause Garbo anguish and anxiety. Still, she could hardly recount her life without describing the people who had played important roles in it.

Her fears were well-founded. While her book said many flattering things about Garbo, it also sounded somewhat patronizing. Several passages gave the impression that Garbo had been the pursuer rather than the pursued. And if Garbo had indeed told her about her childhood and adolescence, Mercedes was one of the few so privileged and that disclosure could be viewed as a betrayal of confidence.

No matter what the content of the book, the result would probably have been the same. From her court Garbo banished Mercedes, who died in 1967, still not restored to favor.

Rouben Mamoulian entered Garbo's life when he was chosen to direct *Queen Christina*. He was born in the Caucasus, and received his education in Moscow and Paris before going on to London and a career as a stage director. He came to the United States in 1923. From the Eastman Theatre in Rochester he moved on to a successful career on the Broadway stage. The advent of sound brought him to Hollywood. There he developed a reputation for technical innovations in such early sound films as *Applause, Dr. Jekyll and Mr. Hyde,* and *Love Me Tonight.*

Garbo responded well to Mamoulian's direction and to his forceful personality. He was thirty-five, eight years her senior. With his bushy black hair and dark horn-rimmed glasses, he looked at once arty and erudite.

To the delight of the columnists and reporters—an astonishing brigade of four hundred regularly stationed in Hollywood during this period—Mamoulian and Garbo went out on the town. They were seen dining together, dancing at the popular clubs on the Sunset Strip. Mamoulian was no John Gilbert, but the four hundred did their best, spreading rumors of engagement and marriage. And indeed, at times the courtship seemed ardent, extending to the periphery of jealousy.

When Mamoulian came to pick Garbo up in his car, she would throw herself on the floor as he passed through the gate. "I will not drive this car out the gate until you behave like a human being," he said one day.

"But I don't want her to see me," said Garbo. A woman suitor, it appears, was pacing up and down outside the gate.

Mamoulian and Garbo made one sortie toward the Grand Canyon which the pursuing press suspected might turn into a honeymoon trip. So numerous and persistent were the newshounds that the beleaguered couple turned back. Mamoulian's Slavic ego reacted poorly to the situation. The romance did not long survive the film's completion.

Queen Christina, enthusiastically received by the critics, was only a modest commercial success. Mamoulian was later interviewed by *Sight and Sound* on the subject of the film's powerful final scene, when the queen stands at the prow of the ship carrying her away to foreign exile.

"Garbo asked me, 'What do I play in this scene?' Remember, she is standing there for a hundred fifty feet of film—ninety of them in closeup. I said, 'Have you heard of tabula rasa? I want your face to be a blank sheet of paper, the writing to be done by every member of the audience. I'd like it if you could avoid blinking your eyes, so that you're nothing but a beautiful mask. So in fact there is *nothing* on her face, but everyone who has seen the film will tell what she is thinking and feeling. And always it's something different. Each one writes his own ending to the film.'"

Observers have often noted that Garbo on the

screen was able to convey a passivity which made it possible for her audiences to read many different thoughts into her expression. It is interesting that Mamoulian consciously strove for this effect in *Queen Christina's* classic final scene.

The earthbound Garbo also meant many things to many people. After her liaison with Mamoulian ended, she embarked on a vastly different adventure, with a man as famous in his field as she was in hers.

Like everyone else, Leopold Stokowski wanted to meet Garbo when he came to Hollywood in 1937. He was fifty-five, twice married, with three children. He had built a towering reputation as conductor of the Philadelphia Symphony Orchestra; now moviegoers were to see his expressive hands and his shock of fluffy white hair on the screen in *Big Broadcast of 1937* and the Deanna Durbin picture, *100 Men and A Girl.*

Anita Loos arranged the introduction to Garbo, now thirty-two, and Stokowski plunged straight into high-toned courtship. Their liaison was written in the stars, he said; they could make a historical pair, like Richard Wagner and his Cosima. His specific artistic aim reportedly was to pair himself with Garbo in *Tristan and Isolde.* The voices would have had to be dubbed, since Garbo's was throaty and low and the maestro's closer to a falsetto.

The film never got off the ground, but the romance did. Stokowski and Garbo made the rounds of Hollywood nightspots where they danced the rhumba into the early hours. The second Mrs. Stokowski embarked for Reno. And once again editors told their outside men not to come back without a photo or an interview with Garbo.

Jim Simmons of the Los Angeles *Examiner* was more persistent than the rest. He waited outside Garbo's house for long hours, and when she took out her car he followed after. She caught on and accelerated. The chase led to George Cukor's mansion on Doheny. Garbo rushed from her car and almost made it to the door before Simmons intercepted her.

"How did you find me?" she asked. "Did you follow me from my house?"

"Yes."

"How sad. How sad."

"Miss Garbo, are you going to marry Mr. Stokowski?"

"No, no, I will not marry Mr. Stokowski. I won't deny that Mr. Stokowski and I are very good friends, but as for marriage to him—no. That is out of the question."

The two good friends kept the wire services of the western world humming when they rendezvoused in Europe. For a month they stayed at the Villa Cimbrone near Ravello in Italy. The press and photographers stalked their every move, much in the manner of the paparazzi around Elizabeth Taylor and Richard Burton's villa several decades later. The dispatches were hardly world-shaking. The modern Wagner and his Cosima ate their diet food and did their yoga exercises, clearly convinced that early to bed and early to rise would make them healthy and wise. They were already wealthy.

The pursuers found it more difficult to follow the trail when the pair left for North Africa. Later there was

a motor tour across the continent, and a sojourn in
Sweden. Then Stokowski returned home alone, followed
some time later by Garbo. On shipboard Garbo surprised everyone by granting an interview.

Was it true that she had gone to see a child born
aboard ship? they asked.

"Yes, I am always interested in babies," she said.

"Would you like children of your own, Miss
Garbo?'

"No. The world now seems too difficult. I would
not want to raise a son or any children to go to war.
But I don't want to say any more about that. I don't
know about politics."

"Did you enjoy your vacation?"

"You cannot have a vacation without peace and you
cannot have peace unless you are left alone."

"Are you already married to Mr. Stokowski?"

"I wish you wouldn't ask me that. I'm afraid if I
were married, you would know all about it."

"Do you ever plan to marry?"

"If I could find the right person to share my life with
perhaps I would marry."

"Do you think single blessedness the proper state for
a professional woman?"

"If you are blessed, you are blessed, whether you are
married or single."

Garbo and Stokowski never became the Wagner and
Cosima of their time. He returned to his conducting
and later married Gloria Vanderbilt. She returned to
her work, and to another health fanatic.

Gayelord Hauser was born in Germany, the eleventh

in a family of twelve children. At sixteen he came to the United States, where he developed a case of tuberculosis viewed pessimistically by his doctors. Dr. Benedict Lust, a specialist in "living" foods, took over Hauser's case and put him on a special diet. Soon, he was cured. Hauser set about spreading this new gospel enthusiastically.

"Wonder foods" like brewer's yeast, powdered skim milk, potassium soup, yogurt, wheat germ, blackstrap molasses, fortified milk, and amino acids were at the foundation of the system he espoused. A regimen of the mind was added to that of the body. In a book entitled *Look Younger; Live Longer*, Hauser encouraged readers to "balance your personality, balance your mind, balance your activities, balance your emotions, balance your marriage, balance your recreation, balance your budget. . . .

"I will teach you how to eat not merely to satisfy hunger but to eat for health, good looks, youth, vitality, the joy of living. I will show you that you are not old at forty, fifty, sixty, seventy. That you need not be old at eighty, ninety. . . . shall I go on?"

His promises were enticing, especially to aging millionaires in fashionable spas and to movie stars whose fortune was in their appearance. Hauser's disciples included famous and fabulous people, among them Lady Elsie Mendl, Clara Bow, and Mercedes D'Acosta. It was Mercedes who introduced him to Garbo, who became the most famous disciple of them all.

The Hauser mixture of packaged and natural sunshine appealed to Garbo. The two took long walks and enjoyed healthful picnics, interspersed with teas at the homes of the rich. The dietitian gave the actress a diamond ring. When they left together for Florida in February of 1940, the newspapers talked of marriage.

As it turned out, Hauser was far from being as publicity-shy as his companion. It was he who gave the marriage story to a friend at a news bureau and said he would confirm, giving him a scoop, when the ceremony was over. The marriage never took place. The entire affair cooled. No doubt Garbo was displeased with Hauser's casual references to her at his lectures and in his books.

Talk of romance ended, but over the years the companionship has been renewed. Today Garbo is a guest at the Hauser home when she visits Hollywood. For two hours each day they walk the fire path between Coldwater Canyon and Laurel Canyon. She refers to him as "Dr. Gay"; to Hauser she is "Miss Gay."

Garbo's loves and friendships in Hollywood spanned the last half of the twenties and the entire decade of the thirties. At the zenith of her career her renown was international, her salary up to $270,000 per picture. Ironically, however, a number of Garbo pictures lost a good deal of money in the United States. MGM was happy to have her nonetheless. She was a prestige showcase for the studio, and her foreign popularity was enormous, moving most of her films into the financial plus column.

Box-office trouble at home began fairly early in the thirties. *Queen Christina* won vast critical acclaim, but fans did not rush to see it. The following year, *The Painted Veil* did even less well. "Guessing Time for Garbo" and similar titles headed magazine articles which now speculated on her retirement. Fifth in popularity in 1933, Garbo dropped to thirty-fourth in 1934.

There were resurgences of box-office power, but the overall trend was down. Some speculated that the decline resulted in part from the changing Garbo characterizations. A heavy fatalism overhung many of her efforts; one knew from the early reels that the ending would be tragic. Moviegoers in the Depression thirties preferred Shirley Temple musicals, "screwball" comedies like *Theodora Goes Wild* and *The Awful Truth*, and the sophisticated comic style of *It Happened One Night*.

Garbo had always appealed to both sexes, but as the thirties unreeled she seemed to be losing at least part of her male audience. It was before the age of the computer, and no surveys were made of the proportion of men to women in the audience. But the screen Garbo was certainly turning more aloof and masculine, and in some instances anti-male.

"That's men again," she complains in *Anna Christie*. "Oh, how I hate 'em, every mother's son of 'em."

"I am my own master," she says in *Mata Hari*.

"I will die a bachelor," she says in *Queen Christina*.

The family as an institution was still extremely strong in the thirties. On the screen, the small-town sagas of Andy Hardy had a strong hold on the American public, with their simple problem situations easily solved by a conference of members of the household. Sex roles were unambiguous—the industry code would not permit a husband to be shown in bed with his wife, let alone a mistress. Garbo's characterizations of sexually complex, even ambiguous women certainly were in advance of their time.

In *Ninotchka* Garbo played another strong, masculine role, that of a Communist diplomat. It was welcomed by the critics and to a considerably lesser extent by the public. Still, it was a success, Garbo's last. War broke out in Europe the year of its release and the foreign market started slipping away. Garbo voluntarily asked the studio to reduce her salary to $125,000 per picture.

Metro decided to retailor Garbo to increase her appeal to American audiences, to make her conform to more conventional concepts of womanhood. The long bob was cut short, and Adrian's high-fashion creations gave way to sack frocks. *Two-Faced Woman* was the result, an ill-conceived, badly executed effort to turn Garbo into an American "oomph" girl. Surprisingly, the National League of Decency condemned the hapless film. "It is almost as shocking as seeing your mother drunk," *Time* said in its review.

"I said, when the glamour ends for Garbo it also ends for me," a melancholy Adrian declared. "She has created a type. If you destroy that illusion you destroy her. When Garbo walked out of the studio, glamour went with her and so did I."

The reign of Queen Greta in Hollywood was over. She had never planted her celebrated feet in the cement of Grauman's Chinese Theatre. She had endorsed no products, had never made a color film. She was nominated for an Academy Award three times—in 1929-30 for both *Anna Christie* and *Romance*, in 1937 for

Camille, and in 1939 for *Ninotchka*—but like Charles Chaplin and D. W. Griffith, she was passed by. Not until 1955 did the Academy catch up with Garbo, presenting her with a special Oscar for "a series of luminous and unforgettable performances." The award was made in absentia.

"The strange truth about the greatest star Metro ever had is that Hollywood itself knew as little about her when she left as it did when she first came to America," wrote Alyce Canfield.

Virtually no one, it seems, listened to what Garbo herself had said.

Garbo as an Actress: Comeback?

"My talents fall within definite limitations," Garbo told a friend in the sixties. "I am not a versatile actress."

Characteristically, Garbo's attitude toward her own acting over the years has often been self-deprecatory. Along with the rest of the Swedish colony, she felt the early vamp pictures were dreadful. Her auto-criticism extended as well to later efforts. "Who ever saw Swedes act like that?" she said after watching the much-praised *Anna Christie.*

"I tried to be Swedish but it's so difficult in Hollywood to be allowed to try anything," she said of the highly poetic and artistic *Queen Christina.* "It's all a terrible compromise. There is no time for art. All that matters is what they call box office."

Once her career was over Garbo started going to the Museum of Modern Art to watch her old films. As biographer John Bainbridge has pointed out, she would often refer to her screen self in the third person—"See what she's doing now? . . . Look at her, look at that gown!"

121

At times she would be amused and mimic the lines, which were indeed often quite ludicrous. In *Susan Lenox* she says to Clark Gable: "Rodney, when will this painful love of ours ever die?" In *The Mysterious Lady* co-star Conrad Nagel says: "I come to you in love. I leave —your enemy."

The argument about whether Garbo was a great actress has been going on for forty years. In the earliest days a number of critics took Garbo at her word and roasted her performances. But there were many who, like Robert E. Sherwood, were extravagant in praising her:

"If we have, thus far, conveyed that *The Kiss* is a mediocre picture exceptionally well-directed, that is what we intended," he wrote in 1929 in the old *Life*. "If we have failed to say much about Greta Garbo, that is because we ran out of adjectives two years ago. We have compared her to Duse, Cavallieri, Mrs. Siddons, Helen of Troy, and Venus, and then ground our teeth because we hadn't made it strong enough. When someone invents a foolproof asbestos pencil, we shall order a gross and write a real piece about Greta Garbo, the best actress in the world. And then throw it in the stove as weak, futile, and anemic."

In recent years the various Garbo film festivals have provoked searching analysis from students of the film art. One of the most famous was Kenneth Tynan's 1954 article in *Sight and Sound* with its oft-quoted line: "What, when drunk, one sees in other women, one sees in Garbo sober." In the piece, Tynan could not resist repeating the "old, hilarious slander which whispered [Garbo] was a brilliant female impersonator. . . . Behind the dark glasses, it was said, there lurked the features of a proud Scandinavian diplomat."

Tynan then spelled out his own view: "She is a woman apprehended with all the pulsing clarity of one of Aldous Huxley's mescalin jags. To watch her is to achieve direct cleansed perception of something which, like a flower or a fold of silk, is raptly, unassertively, and beautifully itself. Nothing intrudes between her and the observer except the observer's neurosis. Her contribution is calm and receptiveness, an absorbent repose which normally in women exists only with the utmost vanity. . . .

"It looks as if we're never to know whether or not Garbo was a great actress," Tynan concluded with more severity than his earlier rhapsody would have led one to expect. "Do I not find the death scene of *Camille* or the bedroom-stroking scene of *Queen Christina* commensurate with the demands of great acting? On balance, no. The great actress, as Gilbert Lowes declares, must show her greatness in the highest reaches of her art; and it must be counted against Garbo that she never attempted Hedda, or Masha, or St. Joan, or Medea. We must acclaim a glorious woman who exhibited herself more profoundly to the camera than any of her contemporaries; but the final accolade must, if we are honest, be withheld."

Tynan's closing point is interesting but one wonders if it is altogether sound. The roles he mentions were all vehicles of great stage actresses, and Garbo's entire career is on film. The two arts are vastly different.

Parker Tyler was one critic who wrote about Garbo in terms of her film art. He did not accept her own view, that she had definite limitations, but rather called her "a fabulous chameleon," with, eventually, "the best trained deportment of anybody then in Hollywood films." He made exception only for certain male comedians, including Charles Chaplin.

Tyler explored at length the sexual image conveyed by Garbo. He referred to her "monosyllabic pelvis," to her "arrestingly ambivalent sort of sexuality," to the "long, poetically prehensile arms of a growing youth." He then hastened to point out that he meant simply that "she just naturally appealed to men, women, and children alike," and that "a magical exemption hovers about the head of anyone, no matter of which sex, of whom that can truly be said." Garbo the chameleon, Tyler said in his essay, was "every inch an actress," and "her destiny was to contribute an actress-personality to the films."

Was she a great actress or just a great screen personality? Richard Whitehall, in a much-discussed 1963 issue of *Films and Filming,* called the MGM films of the Garbo era, "tasteless, passionless, wonderful nonentities. . . . Subtract Garbo from most of her films and one is left with nothing." There were exceptions, he said, notably *Queen Christina, Anna Karenina, Camille, Conquest,* and *Ninotchka.* Overall, Garbo became "the idealization, the abstraction, the very incarnation of the romantic woman, her performance always facets of the same personality. . . . All her characters seem to have merged over the years into a super Garbo act.

"By the standards of realism which shape the modern film, Garbo's characters are not real. They are metaphysical rather than actual; they live within themselves taking no heed of the logic of the outside world, but within her conception of them they possessed a wholeness, their lives and destinies are inevitable and complete.

"She spent her formative years, too many, animating cardboard characters through absurd situations, but in her last roles she touched the highest reaches of her art," Whitehall concluded. "She is, I think, a creative artist in the best sense of the term. The world, and certainly the cinema, has been the richer for her presence."

For all his praise, Whitehall sidestepped the question of greatness by using the phrase "a creative artist in the best sense of the term." In the New York *Times Magazine* of September 1965 Hollis Alpert was more specific: "One feels she would have easily outacted and out-starred Elizabeth Taylor, but on the other hand imagine stacking her up against Ethel Barrymore in her prime? Miss Barrymore, I am sure, would have out-emoted and out-throated her. . . . The observer is never sure if she is an actress or something beyond acting, a phenomenon of nature."

Garbo, it is worth noting, came off very well in *Anna Christie,* where she was up against the formidable Marie Dressler. Neither out-emoted or out-throated the other. Garbo's colleagues have in fact been lavish in their praise of her abilities. Bette Davis is one example: "Her instinct, her mastery over the machine, was pure witchcraft. I cannot analyze this woman's acting. I only know that no one else so effectively worked in front of a camera." Foreign players of the caliber of Jean-Louis Barrault echo these sentiments.

It is true, however, that the actors we call great have the ability to lose themselves in the created character, to make us forget their true identity. Geraldine Page comes strongly to mind. Bette Davis, on the other hand, usually remains Bette Davis, as Joan Crawford remains Joan Crawford. And Garbo, we are always aware, is Garbo, magnetically incarnating a role. Greatness, surely, is not one-dimensional. As an actress, Garbo has many of its aspects, but for the moment the critical consensus stops at praise just short of the highest.

"You see they say nice things about me now," Garbo wrote a friend in Sweden at the height of her fame. "But if I sometime make a bad picture, and if I am no longer popular, you will see they will say I am not a good actress, and other bad things as well."

For more than a quarter of a century Garbo, only thirty-six when she left films, has looked warily at comeback proposals. In fact, her initial plan was to leave MGM only temporarily, until the war's end, and then to resume her career. She promised Louis B. Mayer she would come back if he found a good story for her. Mayer hired a number of people to look for properties.

Adela Rogers St. John was one of them. She alone wrote more than four hundred memos to Mayer with ideas for Garbo films, usually running to ten or twelve pages. Mayer sent those he liked to Garbo, then checked with her. On only one of the four hundred did she nibble. The property was *Black Oxen*, by Gertrude Atherton. Corinne Griffith had played it as a silent film. When Garbo expressed interest, Adela developed the idea to about two hundred pages. Garbo still liked it. She went so far as to tell Mayer she would make some tests for the picture. She never did, and Adela feels that she never intended to.

Despite her feeling of letdown when she left Hollywood, Garbo apparently still placed her greatest trust in MGM. Y. Frank Freeman of Paramount says his studio tried more than a dozen times to interest her in properties—among them a Charles Brackett and Billy Wilder version of Molnar's *Olympia*—but never got past the front door. At Twentieth-Century Fox, Darryl Zanuck tried to interest Garbo in the role of the princess in *Anastasia;* she went twice to see the play, then turned down the role. David Selznick wanted her for his proposed production of a life of Sarah Bernhardt, but she demurred. Jack Warner got nowhere with a war story featuring a female collaborator as the lead.

Garbo has in fact consistently turned down stories dealing with war and violence. In 1944 she refused to consider *Women of the Sea,* which was about the invasion of Norway. Several years later she was having a drink with George Cukor and photographer George Hoyningen-Huene.

"How would you like to make a film of *Tosca?*" asked Hoyningen-Huene. "Not as an opera, of course, but just the story."

"I don't want to kill," Garbo said quickly.

"When are we going to make another picture?" Garbo asks whenever she runs into her old director, Clarence Brown.

"When we get the right story," he always replies.

One venture Brown suggested almost came to fruition. He wanted to remake *Flesh and the Devil* as a talkie. Garbo liked the idea. She was twenty-one when she made it in the silent version, playing a woman of forty-five. Brown proposed the remake at a time when Garbo's real age coincided with that of the heroine. MGM executives liked the idea too, but soon they started reworking the story. The German possession in South Africa should be changed to Argentina, where the studio had money tied up. Forget Garbo, they said, and write a treatment with Ava Gardner in mind. On that note, Brown dropped the project.

G. W. Pabst, who directed her in her second film, *The Joyless Street*, saw Garbo in Rome in the forties and broached an idea for her comeback.

"I want to film the story of Ulysses," he said, "and I want you to play the three women foremost in his life, his wife Penelope, Circe the Enchantress, and Calypso. I will make a rough script and show it to you."

Garbo received the script, and Pabst waited eagerly for her reaction."

"I do nothing but sit and spin," she said, dismissing the project.

Walter Wanger, the producer of *Queen Christina*, came closest to bringing off the coup of a Garbo comeback. In the late forties Garbo expressed definite interest in a screen treatment of the life of Georges Sand. Salka Viertel was the prospective writer, George Cukor was to direct, and Laurence Olivier to co-star. Unfortunately, combined financing by French, British, and American interests grew too complicated and the venture broke down.

A second Wanger project, initiated by producer Eugene Frenke, actually went into the first stages of

production. Balzac's novel *The Duchesse of Langeais*
was the property. Max Ophuls was to direct, James
Mason to be the co-star. William Daniels, Jimmy Howe,
and an Italian cameraman made color tests of Garbo and
these were felt to be superb. Garbo agreed to a salary
of only $50,000 plus a percentage of the film. Frenke,
Wanger, and Garbo went to Italy, where the picture was
to be made. Again, at the last moment, the intricate
multi-national financing fell through.

Principals in the venture have given conflicting accounts of Garbo's role in the debacle. James Mason
gave his to Arkadin of *Sight and Sound:* "Apparently
Garbo insisted on complete incognito while staying at
the largest and most obtrusive hotel, having her very
large and obtrusive car drive 'unobtrusively' to the back
door, and then appearing wearing her unmistakable hats
and dark glasses. And she didn't see the potential finan-
ciers for weeks and weeks, then finally received them
in a darkened suite with all the blinds down, where they
couldn't see her, only to dismiss them after half an hour.
So they got fed up, withdrew their finance, and the film
was never made. A pity in a way, I suppose.

"Of course when you look at Garbo's old films you
realize that she was never really a very good actress
but had that extraordinary ambiguous personality, like
nothing else on film."

Wanger late said that Garbo was completely co-
operative throughout, that Mason's statement was simply
one more in the series of misunderstandings people have
about Garbo; since she has never bothered to deny false-
hoods, they have persisted.

"Out of the question," was his reaction to the prospect of a Garbo comeback, but second thoughts prevailed: "If she found the right story, and the right director, and . . . but all the circumstances would have to be perfect."

Friends in New York say that Garbo was heartbroken over the Italian fiasco. She continued to entertain new proposals thereafter, but with a far more skeptical eye. Nunnally Johnson wanted her for Daphne Du Maurier's *My Cousin Rachel*. Garbo's initial interest abated as they talked of such matters as the danger of certain camera angles. Finally she said no. Designer Norman Bel Geddes wanted her to play the madonna in *The Miracle*, the great Max Reinhardt stage success. Again there were a number of discussions before the final no. John Gunther met Garbo and prepared a scenario about a beautiful lady spy; Garbo read it and told Gunther and MGM it would be ideal for Greer Garson. *Miss Julie*, *Mourning Becomes Electra*, Duse, Bernhardt, Helena Modjeska, Mother Cabrini, Anna Lucasta, Madame Curie, Madame Bovary, Talleyrand, Cyrano de Bergerac, Joan of Arc, and Salome were said to be on the agenda at different times. Even St. Francis entered the lists. When he did, Garbo's friend Aldous Huxley asked, "What? Replete with beard?"

The untrod comeback trail winds into the sixties. Garbo has been approached with offers of a radio show which would feature excerpts from her films plus original story material. She has received fabulous offers from television. Film producer Ross Hunter relayed an offer for her to appear in a Civil War drama called *The Heaven Train*. Garbo has even been rumored ready to play her own life in a film.

One of her close friends is Nadea Loftus, the sister of singer Jessica Dragonette. "I'm sure she'll make another picture," says Nadea. "Garbo is always standing in the wings. Health preoccupies her, and she keeps up her daily beauty routines. Many of the comeback projects broke down through no fault of hers.

"Once, we learned that Robert Edmond Jones wanted her to do *The Juggler of Notre Dame* at Central City. I went to the library and got material on it and she became immersed in it. We were in a little shoe shop one day. She had ordered shoes and they were too tight and she wanted to leave with them as they were —she hates to make a fuss. I said no and went outside, and told the man. When I returned, there was Garbo in front of the mirror practicing scenes from *The Juggler*, twisting her hat this way and that, very Chaplinesque. I'm sure she'll make another picture."

A recent episode is less encouraging. William Frye, the sensitive young producer of television's *The Halls of Ivy*, wanted Garbo for the lead role in a film to be based on the novel *Life with Mother Superior*. She invited him to send her the script. The role of a nun would be ideal for her comeback. Frye felt, providing a smooth transition from the Garbo past to the present. Columbia was willing to pay her one million dollars for a ten-week shooting schedule, plus all expenses. Since Frye knew that Garbo liked his house, next door to Gayelord Hauser, he offered it to her. No inducement was sufficient to lure her back to the screen. Frye made the film, naturally quite altered, with Rosalind Russell.

So long as Garbo is alive, there will be producers and impresarios importuning her to return to the screen.

She will probably continue to flirt with their ideas, but no more than that. The Garbo of the past, the legendary Garbo, is an entity fully formed. Any addition to it would involve great risk. Garbo is too wise to tamper with history's favorable response to her.

The Garbo Court

AFTER LEAVING HOLLYWOOD in the early forties, Garbo waited many years before returning even for a visit. In New York she rented a furnished suite at the Ritz-Tower Hotel, then moved into the Hampshire House. Eventually she settled in an apartment. Admirers and newshawks continued to pursue her—she fled, as before.

With her own incomparable sense of counterpoint, she moved in ever wider circles and yet maintained an aura of seclusion. International high society, even presidents and kings received her. Garbo herself, of course, was modern royalty.

As in every court, there were rituals, some of them elaborate. These had the effect of feeding the legend. Garbo began referring to herself in the plural—"We are very sad today." She telephoned frequently from her New York apartment, but anyone calling in had to know the signal. For a time it was ring twice, hang up, and double ring again. Whenever the code fell into the wrong hands, it was changed.

Over the years, protocol has dictated the form of address. Old friends like Charlie Chaplin call her "Greta," but this salutation is rare. "G.G." is used by those closest to her, and "Miss G" by those who know her less well. Even more distant acquaintances are reduced to "Miss Garbo." An entire category prefers the neutral fiction of "Miss Brown"—Garbo still enjoys this and sometimes announces herself on the telephone as "Miss Brown."

The most important rule of the court decrees that those who frequent it must not talk about the queen. "The conspiracy of silence," it was once called by Harry Crocker. Crocker knew Garbo well, and although it was his business to write about celebrities he never mentioned her in his column. "Garbo works with her friends much on the theory of the underground—one cell doesn't know the next," said Crocker. "She never talks to her friends about any of her other friends."

"We don't want to drop Garbo, and talking about her is the equivalent of dropping her," Eustace Seligman said when asked to comment on Garbo for this book.

"Over the years I have made it a flat policy not to write or talk about Garbo at all," said John Gunther.

"I have been asked a hundred times to talk about Greta Garbo but I never have," said Minna Wallis, her one-time agent. "Ever since she was a child she has placed a high value on her privacy and I respect that. It's why we've been friends for thirty years. It's not a phase with her, she's always been that way."

"It's taboo,' said dress designer Enrique Medina. "I can tell you nothing. It would be the end of us. If anyone talks to you about Garbo, take it with a grain of salt.

They may not know her that well. The people who do don't talk. It's her condition for friendship."

"I'll see you but don't mention my name," said a round dozen people.

When Nathaniel Benchley was writing a piece about Garbo for *Collier's* he, too, came up against the conspiracy of silence and against a number of people willing to talk only on condition that their names be withheld. "Desire for anonymity is not an infallible indication of intimacy," Benchley tartly concluded.

The conspiracy of silence was respected only on the surface. By asking friends not to discuss her, Garbo predictably caused each scrap of news to spread with the four winds. Her friends never stopped talking about her, as the pages of this book attest. Many who will not speak directly for publication leak information and anecdotes to journalists and biographers.

Garbo has continued to mete out punishment to those she has apprehended. In the forties she became a frequent visitor at the New York Museum of Modern Art's film department, and a friend of Allen Porter, the film curator. He would alert the staff to her arrival: "Miss Brown is here." Later the password became simply, "*She's* here."

Near the end of his tenure at the museum, Porter purchased an old deserted church in Barrytown, a small village in upstate New York. He painted the building red and furnished it handsomely. One feature was a Garbo room, filled with fine paintings complemented by portraits of Garbo.

Porter always called his guest "Miss G." She called him "Mr. Porter." It was to Porter that she made the revealing comment, "I never said I want to be alone. I only said I want to be *let* alone." When this remark and others appeared in the Bainbridge biography, Garbo was outraged. Porter was a false friend, she said; like everyone else, he used her. He pointed out that he could hardly have used her, as he had gained nothing from the book. Garbo was unbending. Several years passed before she relented and renewed the relationship.

Paul Mathias, a New York based writer for *Paris-Match*, came to know Garbo well, through Cecile de Rothschild. When a Garbo film festival in France broke suddenly into the news, *Paris-Match* hurriedly prepared an article and showed it to Mathias. He disapproved because it spoke at length of Garbo's frequent companion George Schlee, pointing out that Schlee and Garbo took adjoining rooms when traveling and lived in New York in the same apartment building, where Garbo spent more time in his suite than in her own. When Mathias insisted that this emphasis be changed, he was asked to do an article of his own.

Mathias wrote an account of her daily life which to him seemed innocuous. He described her apartment. He mentioned that she usually went to bed early, sometimes at nine-thirty. That some nights she slept well, others not. Occasionally she took a pill. She liked her charwoman but made her own breakfast so that she was already out of the apartment when the charwoman arrived at eight-thirty. She was bright, and could be very funny. She was at her best from four-thirty in the afternoon to eight. Then she had her first vodka of the day, relaxed and became very amusing.

Mathias tried to check his piece with Garbo, but

she was out of town and could not be reached. *Paris-Match* ran it under the title "Greta Garbo Today."

Garbo saw the account and complained of betrayal to Cecile de Rothschild—Mathias had, among other things, given her street address. She never wanted to see him again. If she knew he would be at a gathering, she would *not* go. She even excused herself from a boat trip because she discovered Mathias would be aboard. One friend who knew that the article said only pleasant, rather bland things about Garbo and her daily routine made a comment: "Maybe that's just what she doesn't want."

The remark was indeed apt. In all her years as a screen star, Garbo kept her distance. She lived up to Louis B. Mayer's idea of a star, and that conception came to coincide with her own. Mathias' piece reduced her to a mundane level the legend would never countenance. She might well have preferred the original *Paris-Match* article, in which she cut a far more romantic figure.

Garbo's court has its rules and regulations, but to enforce them there is only Garbo herself, and as a consequence they are only moderately effective. Her reading—even about herself—is likely to be cursory. She merely glanced through Bainbridge's and Mercedes d'Acosta's books. She may have read Mathias' account in *Paris-Match,* or only heard about it from a friend.

Garbo can, after all, punish only those infractions of court rules which come to light. This is probably fortunate, for her circle would be small indeed if she were more thorough.

George Schlee, the subject of the expunged *Match*

article, might have had to go if Garbo had happened
upon a certain issue of *Time*. It described her relationship with Schlee and his wife Valentina as "a very
European *menage à trois*." Schlee was quoted as saying
to his wife about Garbo: "I love her but she will never
want to get married, and anyway you and I have so
much in common."

Despite this and other comments in print, Schlee's
relationship with Garbo settled into one of the most
meaningful in her life, extending over more than a
quarter of a century. Schlee reminded some people of
Mauritz Stiller. His features and his huge hands were
striking, and he showed a dramatic flair for the art of
living. As a young man in Europe he had married the
lovely, dark-haired Valentina, bringing her to America
in 1927. There were several difficult years before Valentina set up her own dress business, becoming highly
successful in the fashion field.

Gayelord Hauser took Garbo to Valentina to buy
some clothes, and there she met husband and wife. Garbo
was added to their list for dinners and small parties, and
soon the relationship became a matter of public speculation. The three were often seen together, but as frequently Garbo and Schlee were seen alone—especially
after she purchased her seven-room cooperative apartment on New York's East Fifty-Second Street, in the
same building where the Schlees lived.

Once Schlee entered her life, Garbo deferred constantly to him. Other male escorts found themselves relegated to the second rung, often to their annoyance.
Garbo had a habit of calling up and asking to see a

Broadway show, invariably the hottest ticket in town. Had she allowed her escort to say who the tickets were for, they would have been readily available. This she refused to do, fearing that if word got out she would be mobbed at the theatre. She also refused to let tickets be ordered in advance. "I don't know how I'll feel next week," she would say, adding, "And George may want to do something."

Valentina, a witty, entertaining woman, allowed the complex situation to go its own way. Garbo attended her openings, and Valentina's business certainly did not suffer from their association. Many friends saw a strong resemblance between Valentina and Garbo, heightened on occasion when the two appeared in public with Schlee, both wearing the same hairstyle and almost identical costumes designed by Valentina.

In early October of 1964 Garbo and Schlee took adjoining suites at the Hotel Crillon in Paris. After an evening out visiting nightspots, Schlee died in his sleep of a heart attack.

The French magazine *Cine* later reported that at Schlee's death Valentina strongly reasserted herself. She refused to allow Garbo on the plane which brought the body home to New York, and barred her from the funeral. "Le Roc," which everyone assumed was Garbo's villa, turned out to be in Schlee's name, the documentation giving Garbo title missing. Valentina went there, said *Cine*, and destroyed photos and other reminders of the liaison, including valuable antiques Schlee had bought for Garbo.

Today Valentina and Garbo still live in the same

New York apartment house. Friends say Garbo has tipped the elevator man—not even by chance does she wish to run into Valentina.

Garbo has had a sizable circle of courtiers in addition to Schlee. A self-styled "bachelor," she naturally gravitated toward single people whose lives had some of the same flexibility of her own. One of these was the Baron Erich Goldschmidt-Rothschild, a debonair man of the world whom she saw frequently in the years immediately following her retirement. Normally articulate, even garrulous, the Baron was never available for comment on Garbo.

The two made a handsome pair as they strode down the avenue. Garbo usually wore low-heeled shoes and casual but tasteful clothes, including one of her repertoire of floppy hats. The Baron, more than twenty years her senior, was dashing. Swinging a cane, sporting a neatly trimmed white moustache, he was most easily recognizable by the crushed felt hat he wore at a rakish angle. Together they would attend auctions, or stop by antique dealers, or walk in Central Park.

When Garbo learned that the Baron had never seen *Camille*, she took him to the Museum of Modern Art to view it in the private projection room. The Baron seemed to enjoy it. At the end, after the poignant death scene, a museum official asked Garbo her opinion. "It stands up well, doesn't it?" she said. "But it lasts too long."

The question of romance between Garbo and the Baron inevitably came up. "That beautiful creature, don't disappoint me by telling us you're not having an affair," a friend said to Garbo.

"We walk," she replied to her friend, himself a handsome young man.

Before his exile, Allen Porter brought Garbo to William Baldwin's for several memorable Christmas dinners in the late forties. Baldwin, on the threshold of a brilliant career as an interior designer—Jacqueline Kennedy became his most celebrated client—lived in Amster Yard, a charming brownstone on East Forty-ninth Street. Also present at the holiday gatherings were dancer John Butler and Woodson Taulbee, later president of a firm specializing in inventive wallpaper designs. On the first of these occasions Garbo arrived hatless, wearing a simple black dress. The living room faced south, with two tall windows that reached to the floor. It was a sunny day, and a wonderful light bathed the courtyard.

"Will you please draw the curtains and light the candles?' she asked. Baldwin, surprised, turned the sunny day into artificial night.

There was champagne, vodka, caviar, cold turkey and other sandwiches. The dinner was so successful that the following year it was repeated. Again the sun shone, and again Garbo asked for the curtains to be drawn.

"But why in New York, where one sees the sun so little, where so few rooms have this exposure, do you want to draw the curtains?" asked Baldwin.

"It reminds me of Christmases I spent as a child in Sweden," said Garbo. "There it was dark. There was no sunlight."

Garbo and Baldwin worked together decorating her bedroom, and she was pleased with the result. When Baldwin did Cole Porter's suite in the Waldorf Towers, it created something of a sensation. Garbo was eager to see it, and Baldwin offered to take her. The only problem was Cole Porter. Garbo was shy at the thought of meeting the witty composer. Twice luncheon was arranged and each time she broke the date.

"Couldn't we do it when he's at the doctor?" she suggested.

"That wouldn't be nice, Miss G."

Garbo never laid eyes on the suite, although eventually she did meet Cole Porter.

In her autobiography, Elsa Maxwell describes Porter's party for Carole Lombard and Clark Gable at the time of their marriage in 1941. When no one was looking, Garbo slipped out of the room after dinner. "I went into the powder room, opened the door, and stood there transfixed with embarrassment," wrote Elsa. "Garbo was staring so intently into the mirror that she did not hear me enter. I have no idea how long she had been studying her reflection, but she shuddered suddenly and buried her head in her arms. Only she could have found a flaw in that exquisite face. Only a woman with a morbid fear of age could have failed to see that time would enhance the beauty of her classic features and magnificent bone structure. She was thirty-five and all she could see were middle-aged roles in her future. Then, as now, she would not mature gracefully—and she never will."

Garbo revealed her fear of aging to Cecil Beaton one day when she arrived at his studio in the Sherry Netherland. "I was walking up Fifth Avenue and I got a piece of dust in my eye and looked at myself in the compact mirror," she said. "I saw that I had grown so old, so old."

For no reason that he can ascertain, William Baldwin has received no summons to the Garbo court in the past decade. As for Beaton, he has been in and out of her favor a number of times. In his published works he has given his impressions of Garbo, alternately harsh and flattering. It is doubtful that either has helped cement the relationship.

"She is not interested in anything or anybody in particular," he once wrote when they were at odds. "And she has become quite as difficult as an invalid and as selfish, quite unprepared to put herself out for anyone. She would be a trying companion, continuously sighing and full of tragic regrets. She is superstitious, suspicious and does not know the meaning of friendship. She is incapable of love."

Other Beaton comments were more flattering. "Of all the women I have ever seen, Miss Garbo is by far the most beautiful," he later wrote. "After our first meeting in Hollywood many years passed before I met her again, but time had only improved her lunar beauty, given her features a more chiseled sensitivity."

Beaton courted Garbo on two continents before settling for friendship. She was a frequent guest at his lovely Queen Anne residence, Redditch House, in the English village of Broadchalke. On one arrival the cook saw Beaton carry Garbo over the threshold. There was no marriage, however. Garbo, friends say, sometimes regrets that she did not take Beaton up at the full tide of their attraction to one another. With him, she eventually relaxed and seemed free to express a wide range of moods.

Close as he was to Garbo, Beaton never asked her to sit for a camera portrait. It was she who came to him one day and hesitatingly started to speak. "If you were not such a grand and elegant photographer . . ." she began, then stopped. He asked her what she wanted. She needed a passport photograph, she said, and did not wish to go out in public for it.

"So it was as a passport photographer that I took photos of the face of this century," said Beaton, "thereby achieving my greatest ambition and crowning my photographic career."

In the early fifties, Garbo came to another friend for the same purpose—George Hoyningen-Huene. She walked into his studio dressed casually and wearing no makeup. "For government only," she remarked as she sat rigid and impassive before the camera. She was dismayed when she saw the results. For a second set she applied makeup, smoothed her hair, and relaxed. The new photos were far better.

"The construction of Garbo's face is amazing," said Hoyningen-Huene. "The spacing of the eyelids and the above lid is very unusual. She puts that one line of makeup on the lower part of the lid. The effect is remarkable.

"Garbo in films learned the great secret of closeups —not to move at all or to move only very little and very slowly. She raises her eyebrow ever so slightly and it is astonishing."

Because she never offered to pay for the passport

photographs, Hoyningen-Huene considered them technically his own property and offered them for sale to
various publications. When they appeared, Garbo felt
she had been used.

As was the case with her fans in the thirties, members
of the Garbo court have by no means all been male.
Ava Gardner had always wanted to meet Garbo, but in
her early years in Hollywood the occasion never arose.
She was herself a star of considerable magnitude when
Louella Parsons called one day in the fifties to say that
Garbo was coming to town. She had once owned the
house next door to Ava's, which was of identical construction, very private. Could she stay with Ava? The
answer was an enthusiastic yes. Garbo arrived, dressed
in a peculiarly assembled costume which included high
heels and a slouch hat.

"I'm Ava Gardner," said her hostess.

"I'm Greta Garbo. Will you show me to my room,
please?" Ava did, somewhat dismayed by Garbo's formal
manner. "We'll have to get rid of this air conditioning,"
Garbo announced a moment later.

"All you do is turn it off."

Ava left the room and went to tell her sister Bea
how disappointed she was by Garbo's coldness. When
Garbo came out to the pool she accepted a vodka and
then sunned herself, not speaking. She had finished her
second vodka when Ava went into the water topless.
Garbo broke her silence.

"What lovely breasts you have," she said.

After another vodka or two, Bea, a fine southern
cook, suggested food.

"No, thank you, I'm on a diet," said Garbo.

Bea disappeared. Soon the smell of fried chicken was in the air, and Bea returned with a heaping platter. She thrust a drumstick at Garbo. "Eat," she said.

Startled, Garbo tasted. There was no difficulty in persuading her to have a second piece, and a third. The hostess had the final word on the Garbo visit, a definite success thereafter.

"She ate a whole fucking chicken," Ava happily reported.

Garbo has been a wandering monarch, traveling far beyond the confines of New York and Los Angeles, becoming a familiar figure at the playgrounds of Great Britain and Europe. Often she stops off in London to visit Cecil Beaton, or Noel Coward, or Beatrice Lillie. A meeting with Princess Margaret led to instant friendship. At villas up and down the Riviera, Garbo has basked in the sun, surrounded by creature comforts and well-placed friends and acquaintances.

In Paris she enjoys shopping with members of the Rothschild family, luncheons and dinners at Maxim's, tours of churches, museums, art galleries. Also on the agenda is Alexandre, the famous hair stylist responsible for Garbo's simple, much-imitated coiffure.

The Continental press called Garbo "The Eternal Vagabond" as she sailed the Mediterranean on spacious yachts after her retirement. One season it was film producer Sam Spiegel's good ship *Malahne*. The next year and for many thereafter it was the yacht of Aristotle Socrates Onassis, a man roughly Garbo's age.

A crew of fifty served on the converted Canadian

frigate which Onassis turned into a floating palace, *The Christina*. In addition to the best foods and wines there was the luxury and beauty of the ship itself. One bathroom was a replica in Sienna marble of that in King Minos' lost palace of Knossus in Crete; flying fish and dolphins were inlaid in exquisite mosaics. El Greco's *Ascension* was only one of a collection of great paintings.

Garbo was often very gay in Onassis' presence. At one Monte Carlo club she sang to the accompaniment of violins. The melody was a Greek song, "Saapair," which translates "I love you."

At home in New York, Garbo's East Side neighbors are well aware of the royal personage living in their midst. They have entered into an unspoken pact to respect her prerogatives. They smile and chat, but only if she initiates the contact; no one calls her by name or imposes on her for an autograph. She is part of the neighborhood—but with a difference. To friends she has confided that she sometimes goes out in the morning and follows people to see what *they're* up to and where they're going. One is reminded of the monarchs of old who sometimes mingled unobtrusively with their subjects, the better to ascertain the mood of the people.

Everyone has a story about seeing Garbo or, for the more fortunate, actually meeting her. One young man alerted all his friends to call him whenever they saw his idol. He would then dash into a taxi and speed to the area. Three times she was gone when he arrived.

One day he was in the notions department of Altman's when an unmistakable voice spoke to him. "Do they still have a closet shop here?" asked Garbo. He mumbled an answer and then dashed for a nearby phone booth, where he sat and waited for his composure to return.

Baldwin Bergersen, the Norwegian composer of *Carib Song* and other musicals, long admired Garbo from afar. One day at D'Agostino's market he was reaching for a grapefruit when *her* hand touched the same fruit. He released the grapefruit.

Bergersen was later elated when two friends of Garbo's offered to invite her to dinner with him. All was arranged. He arrived early. Garbo was late. At eight o'clock the phone rang. It was Garbo, cancelling. "I just can't face a Norwegian this evening," she said in explanation.

Sometimes the adulation has been a bit confused. Garbo and a friend came into an antique shop one day. "That's rather nice," said Garbo, picking up an object. "Do you really like it, Miss Dietrich?" asked the owner. Garbo inspected various other items in the shop. When she turned to go, the woman told "Miss Dietrich" how honored she was to have her come in. Outside, Garbo broke into giggles. "She obviously didn't get a look at my legs," she said.

Garbo is a frequent visitor at many of the stores and shops in Manhattan. At Bloomingdale's, where most shoppers riding the escalators clutch the side guards, Garbo rides the middle of the step, her head high. One woman gazed at her in astonishment. "Are you who I think you are?" she asked. "No," said Garbo.

Garbo often walks past store windows to be sure there are not too many people inside. Other days, she goes into the back and watches work being done. Everywhere she is courteous, thoughtful, well-liked. The manager of the Flea Market offered to give her a discount because she has been so long unemployed; Garbo was amused by the gesture. When she runs into friends at a shop, she sometimes is dismayed. "I look so awful today," she will say. "I don't feel well."

Garbo has been more relaxed in recent years, more at home with life. She has shown an ever-increasing capacity for friendship and for both inadvertently and intentionally perpetuating her legend.

Cecile de Rothschild, daughter of French banker Robert de Rothschild, appears to be her closest confidante today. Their relationship spans a quarter of a century. Garbo visits Cecile at her home in France, and Cecile comes often to New York. On the evening of one leavetaking, a friend saw her bidding goodbye to Garbo under a dim street lamp. Tears were streaming down Garbo's face. The two women have also been known to quarrel, perhaps the most substantial proof of intimacy.

Another Garbo relationship that has lasted for more than twenty-five years is with Jessica Dragonette and her sister Nadea. Jessica made her radio debut when NBC was one month old and was soon reaching sixty-six million listeners weekly. She was the first performer to sing light opera on the air. One of her fans was Garbo. Gayelord Hauser, a friend of the sisters, announced one day that he was bringing Garbo to brunch at the Dragonette apartment on New York's Fifty-seventh Street. In her book *Faith is a Song* Jessica recounts the event:

"A series of half-hourly telephone calls ensued in which Gayelord announced the status quo. Yes, she will come. Then no, don't think she can make it. Again, she has changed her mind. And finally, she will come if you can assure her that no one but yourselves will be there. It all added up to a kind of frenzied suspense until at last I went to the door myself in answer to the bell."

When Garbo arrived she said she wanted only poached eggs and postum. With that she handed the maid, Adelaide, a small pack of postum. Adelaide was indignant. "We have our own postum," she declared.

The spacious and handsome Dragonette apartment, designed decades ago by Arthur Gordon Smith and McClelland Barclay, has been a gathering place for a wide circle of friends. Naturally there have been names from music such as Oscar Levant, John Charles Thomas, James Melton, and George Gershwin. Also on hand one might find poets John Hall Wheelock and Edgar Lee Masters, Screen Gems executive Harry Ackerman, Bishop Fulton Sheen, or columnist Dorothy Kilgallen.

Garbo joined the circle, the sisters made up their minds to be detached, not to pry, never to ask questions. As a result, Garbo felt at ease. She was often prankish, full of kidding humor.

"Will you vote for me as President of the United States?" she asked Jessica. "I'm a good man. Besides, I'll have to do something important after having been in the films."

"Everyone who knows Garbo thinks he understands her," Jessica said in her book. "I rather think people misunderstand her natural curiosity, her meticulous thoroughness, her suggestibility. . . . It is her spontaneous ability to act every scene in life, as well as on the screen, that makes her so fascinating."

"If you want to know Garbo, look at her films,"

echoes Jessica's colorful sister Nadea. "She is like that in real life. Supremely she is the actress. She's always on camera."

In the Dragonette household there are beautiful paintings, fine books, recordings by or of Sarah Bernhardt, James Joyce, Edna St. Vincent Millay, Walt Whitman. At a breakfast, Garbo asked for a copy of *Leaves of Grass* and did a beautiful reading of an obscure poem from the volume. Only recently she asked again to hear the Bernhardt and Joyce recordings.

"Garbo is basically extremely honest," says Nadea. "Most people don't understand this. She reads anything and everything, but she never talks about things she doesn't understand thoroughly. She'll say nothing. She can't participate all the time, she's too honest. And so she retreats and people think she's mysterious. The mystery is something that people read into her. Every friend has a completely different veiw of her, that's how complex she is. That's the canvas."

In the sixties, Garbo has continued to be a frequent, favored guest. For several years she has visited on Fire Island, the exotic resort off Long Island which attracts a heavy contingent of people in the arts, many of them emotionally volatile and sexually liberated. In New York she still shows up frequently at parties—at one, Richard Burton met her, asked her if he could kiss her knee, and did so.

In London, Garbo recently attended a large party given by the John Gunthers at Claridge's. She was in good form, but kept moving from the main room toward more intimate groupings elsewhere. Gunther would genially bring her back, each time supplying background notes for the person he wanted her to meet. Sacheverell Sitwell was next on the agenda, he told her at one point, explaining with some pride that he was the brother of Osbert and Edith Sitwell. Garbo dutifullly placed herself in a seat next to Sitwell while Gunther looked on, then asked him "Who are you?"

When possible Garbo still chooses small intimate restaurants or clubs for evenings out. More public appearances continue to produce bedlam. Producer William Frye recently escorted her to a matinee performance of *Funny Girl* in New York. They slipped quietly into house seats, third row on the aisle, just as the curtain went up. By intermission every member of the audience was aware that Garbo was there. Blue-haired matinee ladies surrounded her, testifying to Garbo's continuing appeal to her own sex. "I've loved you forever." "May I touch you?" "You are so beautiful, Miss Garbo." "May I have your autograph?" "Oh, Miss Garbo, how I have loved you!"

As she left the theatre at the end of the show, Frye ran interference on the way to the car. There, determined fans tried to enter from both sides—one was ejected by a policeman. Garbo remained calm throughout, though she was clearly disturbed.

On rare occasions, Garbo herself entertains at her New York apartment. Located at the relatively secluded end of East Fifty-second Street, it has the atmosphere of a small country house in France, with two windows looking out on trees and the East River, several exposures on the south, and a large fireplace on the west wall. The wood-paneled, low-ceilinged room is sunny during the day and the whole impression is rosy—the old brocade curtains, bought at auction, are rose; the furniture, very large but warm Regence, is rose; fresh pink and red carnations are everywhere. The walls of the L, which could be used as a dinette, are covered top to bottom with paintings, many rose-colored or having roses as subject matter.

The largest piece of furniture is a Louis XVth red lounge bed that once belonged to Madame Balsam. This is in a darker part of the room, near the entrance from the hallway, and here Garbo spends much of her time reading or watching television. She has a fine library, including many beautifully bound books from the French eighteenth century. The room is tied together by the warm colors, by a splendid Aubusson rug, and by the many paintings, including one very handsome Renoir which is seldom seen even in reproduction.

Garbo receives her visitors in a cheerful area dominated by one of the southern exposures. Those who have been guests say she is an excellent hostess. No servants are in evidence. Garbo brings forth cheese and Swedish salami if the invitation is for the cocktail hour; she may mix the drinks herself, or, if the guests are men, ask them to help themselves. If dinner has been specified, it may be as simple as cold chicken from a delicatessen. Always the mood will be relaxed and unpretentious.

Entertaining at home, Garbo sometimes startles others by her directness. She has been known to ask an elderly woman whether or not she is a virgin. She will find out what one guest thinks about God, or speculate on the progress of another's romance. On one occasion she was with two homosexuals when a helicopter swung quite low against the night sky outside. "Don't you hope

that there are two beautiful young men up there?"
she asked.

Garbo today is sixty-four. Once all the lines of the
face went up. Now at each corner of the mouth a solitary curve points downward. A network of very fine
lines crisscrosses the skin which, unlike that of so many
of her screen contemporaries, has never been altered by
a plastic surgeon. There is still striking beauty in the
Garbo face, especially when seen in animation. The
classic high cheekbones remain, and the deep-set eyes.
In them there is still *that* look—the look, someone has
said, of one who has a great secret.

Most of Garbo's friends know her as warm and
giving. The public, however, still sees her as a lonely
and aloof woman. In all the years since her retirement
from films, she has never ceased to project this image.
The Garbo court, that unique creation forged by the
will of Queen Greta, has been an effective instrument.
Its standards and stratagems have enabled her to lead,
at least in part, much of the life she wanted.

There are those who continue to wonder if that
life has not been sterile and lonely, but the question
seems parochial, the questioners victims of the mystique
Garbo herself has chosen to keep alive. Greta Garbo
has hardly been life's victim. Her childhood ambition
was to become a movie actress, and on the screen she
achieved a career of incendiary success. As an adult she
chose a way of life, manipulating people and circumstances to accommodate herself and fill it as she wished.

The strictest rule of the Garbo court has been the
ban on discussing her—though if everyone were actually

to stop, she would no doubt suffer agonies. Just as she told Allen Porter "I never said I want to be alone. I only said I want to be let alone," so she would very likely say, "I never said I don't want people to talk about me, I only said I don't want them to talk foolishly about me." "Foolishly" might well include any talk which undermined the mystique. In any case, her proscription has had the one effect which could not fail to amuse her—it has added to the legend. Talk there has been, but forbidden talk, thereby lending further distance to its subject. Garbo, in short, has had her cake and eaten it.

While her court played out the "Don't talk about me" melody, Garbo herself skillfully continued with the contrapuntal "I have nothing to say," which served the same purposes. As a healthy young Swedish girl catapulted to truly outrageous fame, Garbo spoke in earnest when she inveighed against crowds and bemoaned her lost privacy. At the same time, she was from the beginning astute and resourceful at finding ways to cope with her unique set of problems. In her long years of retirement, she made further substantial adjustments. She began to look at her own legend with a wry smile. It is likely that she was well aware of the effect her many cryptic comments had, knew how smoothly they fit the image of a woman removed from obvious modes of feeling.

"I'm just drifting," she told one newspaperman who asked about her plans when she returned to New York from a European jaunt. "I am glad to become a citizen of the United States," she said on becoming a citizen of the United States. "It was awful, simply awful," was her description of a glamorous hegira through the Mediterranean. Asked where she had gone in Greece, she replied, "Oh, I don't know. I think we saw Lesbos."

One can imagine Garbo enjoying each remark. She has seen no advantage in talking to reporters about her trips and so, with listless remarks, she puts them off. Such behavior is hardly peculiar for a woman who has kept her true self to herself and to those who meant something in her life.

"Individual life is tragic," C. P. Snow once wrote. "Man is ineluctably alone and it is a short way to the grave. But believing this, there is no reason why social life should be tragic—it lies within one's power to control, as human loneliness and death do not, and it is contemptible of the false-profound to confuse the two."

Garbo's mystique has confused the two, portraying her only as the romantic symbol of the mysterious and lonely woman. Loneliness can have its charm, and it is true that Garbo has indulged her loneliness. She has, however, never confused life with social life. She has controlled the latter with extraordinary firmness, establishing and following her own rules of conduct. She sees only those she wants to see. She has the strength *not* to pick up the phone. That kind of discipline has over the years forged a ruthless honesty which enables her to deal with the good things in life and also the hectic on her own terms. Only one in a million can do it; we are forced to call such people eccentrics. One of the most striking originals of our time, Garbo is by this definition, or any other, an eccentric.

When her star in Hollywood was at its zenith, *The New Yorker* ran a squib which quoted producer Jerry Wald on the merits of another actress's performance. "She was much better," said Wald. "After all, you can't expect people to be Garbos first time out."

The *New Yorker* comment was brief: "Garbo was."

Appendix: The Films of Greta Garbo

EUROPEAN

1. ADVERTISING SHORTS: Two silent films directed by Captain Ragnar Ring. The first, in 1921, was produced by Hasse W. Tullbergs for Paul U. Bergström's department store in Stockholm. It showed how customers should *not* dress. Greta Gustafsson, in a small comic role, modeled ungainly fashions. In 1922, Ring cast her in a comic short made for the Co-operative Society of Stockholm's Bakery Department. In a restaurant scene and again at a picnic, she gorged herself on rich pastries. Fribergs Filmbrya was the producer.

2. LUFFAR-PETTER (PETER THE TRAMP) A silent comedy in the Mack Sennett tradition; written, directed, and produced by Erik A. Petschler. Premiere: Odeon Theatre, Stockholm, December 26, 1922.

Fire Lieutenant
 Erik Silverjälm *and*
Max August Petterson

(alias Luffar-Petter)	Erik A. Petschler
Greta Nordberg	Greta Gustafsson
Artillery Captain	Helmer Larsson
Police Officer	Fredrik Olsson
Tyra	Tyra Ryman
Mayor's Wife	Gucken Cederborg

STORY: A pompous army fire officer takes the Mayor's three daughters bathing. He falls in love with one, Greta Gustafsson. A series of escapades follows. A passing tramp steals his uniform and impersonates him. The officer ends up marrying a rich widow.

CRITICS: "Since Miss Gustafsson has so far had only the dubious pleasure of having to play a 'Bathing Beauty' for Mr. Erik Petschler in his fire department film, we have received no impression whatever of her capacity. It pleases us, though, to have the opportunity of noting a new name in Swedish films and we hope to have a chance to mention it again. Greta Gustafsson. May perhaps become a Swedish film star. Reason: her Anglo-Saxon appearance."—*Swing* (Stockholm, 1923)

3. THE SAGA OF GÖSTA BERLING (Silent, with English titles, 105 minutes; with French titles, 165 minutes) Directed by Mauritz Stiller. Produced by Svensk Filmindustri. Screenplay by Mauritz Stiller and Ragnar Hlytén-Cavallius. Adapted from the novel by Selma Lagerlöf. Photographed by Julius Jaenzon. Premiere: Röda Kvarn, Stockholm, March 10, 1924.

Gösta Berling	Lars Hanson
Majorskan Samzelius	Gerda Lundeqvist
Major Samzelius	Otto Elg-Lundberg
Melchior Sinclaire	Sixten Malmerfelt

Gustafva Sinclaire	Karin Swanström
Marianne Sinclaire	Jenny Hasselqvist
Countess Martha Dohna	Ellen Cederström
Countess Ebba Dohna	Mona Mårtenson
Count Henrik Dohna	Torsten Hammersen
Countess Elizabeth	
Dohna	Greta Garbo

STORY: Gösta Berling, a defrocked minister, becomes a tutor in the house of an important family and there meets Italian Countess Elizabeth Dohna. Her love eventually redeems him but not before several spectacular scenes, including the burning of the family mansion and a chase across the ice with howling wolves in pursuit.

CRITICS: "Stiller's discovery, Greta Gustafsson, is a trifle plump and unbecomingly costumed. Her fresh young face appears attractive, but her beauty is not fully exhibited until the dramatic night scene when Gösta takes her on his sled across the frozen lake. Dressed in a fur coat, her loose, frizzy hair hidden under a hat, suddenly, when she turns her head to Gösta as the lake glistens and the dark firs and mountains flash by, she becomes GARBO—cool, almost philosophic, frightened, yet carried away by love. We see that shimmering face, that ethereal look, that fineness of expression for the first time in all their beauty. One would not have to be a demonic hero or a ravenous wolf to want to pursue her."—Arthur Lennig, Museum of Modern Art Garbo Festival (1968).

4. DIE FREUDLOSE GASSE (THE JOYLESS STREET) (Silent, 90 minutes) Directed by Georg Wilhelm Pabst. Produced by Sofar-Film. Screenplay by Willi Haas. Adapted from the novel by Hugo Bettauer. Photography by Guido Seeber. Premiere: Mozartsaal, Berlin, May 18, 1925.

Councillor Franz Rumfort	Jaro Furth
Butcher of Merchior St.	Werner Krauss
Maria Lechner	Asta Nielsen
Greta Rumfort	Greta Garbo
Frau Greifer	Valeska Gert
Lieutenant Davy	Einar Hanson
Regina Rosenow	Agnes Esterhazy
Rosa Rumfort	Loni Nest
Egon Stirner	Henry Stuart
Don Alfonzo Canez	Robert Garrison
Lia Leid	Tamara

STORY: The scene is Vienna after World War One; the theme, postwar decadence and corruption. Garbo plays the eldest daughter of an impoverished family she is trying to hold together. Tempted by prostitution, she is saved by an officer of the American Red Cross.

CRITICS: "In *Joyless Street* Garbo is all that a film star in the making should be. Just as it is only her eyes that are finished, so her acting is only first-class in the emotional passages. She is gawky as well as glamorous. But even in those days Garbo had that indefinable something which draws your eyes to one unbroken filly in the field and keeps you from looking at all the others."—James Agate (1935)

AMERICAN

1. THE TORRENT (Silent, 75 minutes) Directed by Monta Bell. Produced by Metro-Goldwyn-Mayer. Screenplay by Dorothy Farnum. Adapted from the novel by Blasco-Ibañez. Photographed by William Daniels. New York Premiere: Capitol Theatre, February 21, 1926.

Don Rafael Brull	Ricardo Cortez
Leonora	Greta Garbo
Remedios	Gertrude Olmstead
Pedro Moreno	Edward Connelly
Cupido	Lucien Littlefield
Doña Bernardo Brull	Martha Mattox
Don Andreas	Lucy Beaumont
Doña Pepa	Tully Marshall

STORY: Leonora and Rafael grow up in the same Spanish village and become sweethearts. Rafael's domineering mother, a local aristocrat, decides that Leonora is not good enough for her son. Leonora is sent to Paris, where she becomes a celebrated prima donna. When she returns to her native village the love affair resumes, but the mother again separates them. Rafael marries his mother's choice; Leonora loses herself in her career. The emotional misery engulfing the principals was to form the prototype for the "Garbo ending."

CRITICS: "Miss Garbo was clothed in a series of the most improbably hideous garments ever conceived by the human mind.

"She was beautiful then, but not as she is now. . . . Her hair was darker, her face more fully rounded, her eyes less wholly unreal. In her acting, she sketched in what she is now, but only sketched it."—Joseph Alsop (1935)

2. THE TEMPTRESS (Silent, 95 minutes) Direction begun by Mauritz Stiller, with final two-thirds completed by Fred Niblo. Produced by Metro-Goldwyn-Mayer. Screenplay by Dorothy Farnum. Adapted from the book by Blasco-Ibañez. Photographed by Tony Gaudio. New York Premiere: Capitol Theatre, October 10, 1926.

Robledo	Antonio Moreno
Elena	Greta Garbo
Manos Duros	Roy D'Arcy
Monsieur Fontenoy	Marc McDermott
Canterac	Lionel Barrymore
Celinda	Virginia Brown Faire
Torre Blanca	Armand Kaliz
Josephine	Alys Murrell

STORY: The wife of a weak-willed South American exercises her wiles on a series of men, a banker, a bandit, and an engineer. Death and disaster follow in her wake, and she ends her days as a streetwalker in Paris.

CRITICS: "Greta Garbo vitalizes the name part of this picture. She *is* the temptress. Her tall, swaying figure moves Cleopatra-ishly from delirious Paris to the virile Argentine. Her alluring mouth and volcanic, slumbrous eyes enfire men to such passion that friendships collapse."—Dorothy Herzog, *The New York Mirror* (1926)

3. FLESH AND THE DEVIL (Silent, 95 minutes) Directed by Clarence Brown. Screenplay by Benjamin Glazer. Adapted from Hermann Sudermann's novel, *The Undying Past*. Produced by Metro-Goldwyn-Mayer. Photographed by William Daniels. Edited by Lloyd Nosler. New York Premiere: Capitol Theatre, January 9, 1927.

Leo Von Sellinthin	John Gilbert
Felicitas Van Kletzingk	Greta Garbo
Ulrich Von Kletzingk	Lars Hanson
Hertha Prochvitz	Barbara Kent
Uncle Kutowski	William Orlamond
Pastor Breckenburg	George Fawcett
Leo's Mother	Eugenie Besserer
Count Von Rhaden	Marc McDermott

STORY: Garbo plays another vamp, the wife of an elderly Austrian count to whom she is blatantly unfaithful. All men are her prey, including two young noblemen whose lifelong friendship she imperils. They face each other in a duel even as she suffers for her sins by drowning under the ice of a frozen river.

CRITICS: "Never before has John Gilbert been so intense in his portrayal of a man in love. Never before has a woman so alluring, with a seductive grace that is far more potent than mere beauty, appeared on the screen. Greta Garbo is the epitome of pulchritude, the personification of passion. . . . Frankly, never in our screen career have we seen seduction so perfectly done."—*The New York Herald Tribune* (1927)

4. LOVE (Silent, 80 minutes) Directed by Edmund Goulding. Produced by Metro-Goldwyn-Mayer. Screeplay by Frances Marion. Adapted from Leo Tolstoy's *Anna Karenina*. Titles by Marion Ainslee and Ruth Cummings. Photographed by William Daniels. Edited by Hugh Wynn. New York Premiere: Embassy Theatre, November 29, 1927.

Anna Karenina	Greta Garbo
Vronsky	John Gilbert
Grand Duke	George Fawcett
Grand Duchess	Emily Fitzroy
Karenin	Brandon Hurst
Seresha, Anna's child	Philippe De Lacy

STORY: Anna Karenina, the wife of a wealthy Russian, falls in love with an army officer. Her husband refuses to give her a divorce, and she becomes the officer's mistress. Eventually realizing that he will return to his career and that she will lose him, she throws herself in front of a moving train.

CRITICS: "Greta Garbo has never been better. In her first
American pictures she was something different from this:
a sensual body, thin and wriggling like an exotic liana, plus
a couple of heavy eyelids that hinted at all kinds of pic-
turesque lusts. But gradually Miss Garbo has worked her
way towards becoming a real artist, an actress with depth
and sincerity. What she gets out of the part of Anna
Karenina, which is far from easy, is always engrossing, often
touching, sometimes even human and great."—Dr. Bengt
Idestam-Almquist (1928)

5. THE DIVINE WOMAN (Silent, no print available)
Directed by Victor Seastrom. Adapted from Gladys Un-
ger's play *Starlight*. Scenario by Dorothy Farnum. Edited
by Conrad Nervig. Photographed by Oliver Marsh. New
York Premiere: Capitol Theater, January 14, 1928.

Marianne	Greta Garbo
Lucien	Lars Hanson
M. Legrande	Lowell Sherman
Mme. Pigonier	Polly Moran
Mme. Zizi Rouck	Dorothy Cumming
Jean Lery	John Mack Brown
Gigi	Cesare Gravina
Paulette	Paulette Duval

STORY: Begun as a life of Sarah Bernhardt, *The Divine
Woman* soon took its own course. Marianne arrives in
Paris and is tempted by her mother's lover, Legrande. She
thwarts him and is befriended by a young soldier, but when
he leaves to join his regiment, she succumbs to Legrande's
offer to make her a great actress. She succeeds on the stage,
but feels remorse when the soldier returns, a deserter. She
leaves Legrande and her career as well. Her fortunes
steadily decline, and she is on the verge of suicide when

the soldier finds her. He carries her off to a small ranch in South America where they begin life anew.

CRITICS: "Many who admit that there is acting on the screen have stated that Miss Garbo did not act, however, that she was only a beautiful woman with a strong appeal. After seeing her play Marianne in this new Metro-Goldwyn picture, no one ever again can say that."—Harriette Underhill, *New York Herald Tribune* (1928)

6. THE MYSTERIOUS LADY (Silent, 90 minutes) Directed by Fred Niblo. Produced by Metro-Goldwyn-Mayer. Screenplay by Bess Meredyth. Adapted from the novel *War in the Dark* by Ludwig Wolff. Titles by Marion Ainslee and Ruth Cummings. Photographed by William Daniels. Edited by Margaret Booth. New York Premiere: Capitol Theatre, August 4, 1928.

Tania	Greta Garbo
Captain Karl Von Heinersdorff	Conrad Nagel
General Alexandroff	Gustav Von Seyffertitz
Colonel Von Raden	Edward Connelly
Max	Albert Pollet
General's Aide	Richard Alexander

STORY: Tania, a Russian spy, is asked to steal military plans from an Austrian officer. She falls in love with him but nonetheless carries out her assignment. The officer is court-martialed and imprisoned. He escapes and goes to Russia to look for her. He finds her and discovers that she truly loves him. Tania double-crosses her superiors and returns with him to Austria to help clear his name.

CRITICS: "None of the actors are able to do much about it,

save to wander through and hope for something better next time. Miss Garbo is pretty, but she doesn't make too good a Russian spy."—Mordaunt Hall, *New York Times* (1928)

7. A WOMAN OF AFFAIRS (Silent, 90 minutes) Directed by Clarence Brown. Produced by Metro-Goldwyn-Mayer. Screenplay by Bess Meredyth. Adapted from the novel *The Green Hat* by Michael Arlen. Photographed by William Daniels. Edited by Hugh Wynn. New York Premiere: Capitol Theatre, January 19, 1929.

Diana Merrick	Greta Garbo
Neville	John Gilbert
Hugh	Lewis Stone
David	John Mack Brown
Geoffrey Merrick	Douglas Fairbanks, Jr.
Sir Montague	Hobart Bosworth
Constance	Dorothy Sebastian

STORY: Diana Merrick, an impetuous, headstrong English girl, falls in love with Neville Montague, but his strait-laced father stops their marriage. She then engages in a series of romantic adventures, culminating in marriage to a charming man who turns out to be a thief. Discovered, he commits suicide. Neville, although himself married, returns to Diana. She sees that their love will ruin his life and sends him away. Despondent, she is thinking of their ill-fated romance as her car crashes into a tree and kills her.

CRITICS: "Miss Garbo saves an unfortunate situation throughout by a subtle something in her playing that suggests just the exotic note that is essential to the whole theme and story. Without her eloquent acting the picture would go to pieces."—*Variety* (1929)

8. WILD ORCHIDS (Silent, 100 minutes) Directed by Sidney Franklin. Produced by Metro-Goldwyn-Mayer. Screenplay by Hans Kraly, Richard Schayer, and Willis Goldbeck. Adapted from the story "Hunt" by John Coltron. Photographed by William Daniels. Edited by Conrad Nervig. New York Premiere: Capitol Theatre, March 30, 1929.

Lillie Sterling	Greta Garbo
John Sterling	Lewis Stone
Prince De Gace	Nils Asther

STORY: Middle-aged John Sterling takes his young wife Lillie with him on a business trip to the Orient. They meet a Javanese prince who later invites them to his palace. When John's duties necessitate his leaving, Lillie and the Prince have an affair. John discovers them, and during a suspenseful tiger hunt Lillie fears that the two men will come to harm over her. Instead, John offers to give her a divorce if that will make her happy. He is about to leave for home when she comes to him, declaring her love for him. They are reconciled.

CRITICS: "Miss Garbo's acting is well-timed and, as usual, effective. It is not an easy role, but she succeeds in imparting to it no small amount of subtlety."—Mordaunt Hall, *The New York Times* (1929)

9. THE SINGLE STANDARD (Silent, 73 minutes) Directed by John S. Robertson. Produced by Metro-Goldwyn-Mayer. Screenplay by Josephine Lovett. Adapted from the novel by Adela Rogers St. Johns. Titles by Marion Ainslee. Photographed by Oliver Marsh. Edited by Blanche Sewell. New York Premiere: Capitol Theatre, July 27, 1929.

Arden Stuart	Greta Garbo
Packy Cannon	Nils Asther

Tommy Hewlett	John Mack Brown
Mercedes	Dorothy Sebastian
Ding Stuart	Lane Chandler
Anthony Kendall	Robert Castle
Mr. Glendenning	Mahlon Hamilton
Mrs. Glendenning	Kathlyn Williams
Mrs. Handley	Zeffie Tilbury

STORY: Debutante Arden Stuart has a long romance with Packy Cannon, a dashing yachtsman and artist. She returns home to San Francisco to find that society frowns on her affair and that she is an outcast. She marries an old admirer, has a child by him, and regains some favor. But when Packy returns, she is once again tempted. Her husband's near-suicide awakens her: realizing that home and child are more important to her than romantic adventures, she renounces Packy.

CRITICS: "For the first time since she hit these shores, grim Greta Garbo has done a good piece of work. In *The Single Standard* she actually walks, smiles, and acts. I have never been able to understand the universal palpitation that has followed her slow but stupid appearance on the great American screen—sex appeal, unfortunately, is a matter of opinion. Nevertheless the lady can, and does, act in her latest movie, and the fact that she is homely and awkward while so engaged only makes me like her more."—Pare Lorentz, *Judge* (1929)

10. THE KISS (Silent, 65 minutes) Directed by Jacques Feyder. Produced by Metro-Goldwyn-Mayer. Screenplay by Hans Kraly. Adapted from an original screen story by George M. Saville. Photographed by William Daniels. Edited by Ben Lewis. New York Premiere: Capitol Theatre, November 15, 1929.

Madame Irene Guarry	Greta Garbo
André	Conrad Nagel
Monsieur Guarry	Anders Randolf
Lassalle	Holmes Herbert
Pierre	Lew Ayres
Durant	George Davis

STORY: Irene Guarry resists the advances of an ardent young admirer, but her husband becomes insanely jealous. When he tries to kill the young man, Irene wrests away the gun and kills her own husband. When she is brought to trial her lawyer, a former lover, secures her acquittal by citing testimony that the husband was despondent over business and probably took his own life. Irene has never told him the true story. After the trial, she goes with him—dreading, however, the revelation she must eventually make.

CRITICS: "If we have, thus far, conveyed that *The Kiss* is a mediocre picture exceptionally well-directed, that is what we intended. If we have failed to say much about Greta Garbo, that is because we ran out of adjectives two years ago. We have compared her to Duse, Cavallieri, Mrs. Siddons, Helen of Troy and Venus, and then ground our teeth because we hadn't made it strong enough. When someone invents a foolproof asbestos pencil, we shall order a gross and write a real piece about Greta Garbo, the best actress in the world. And then, throw it in the stove, as weak, futile and anemic."—Robert E. Sherwood, *Life* (1929)

11. ANNA CHRISTIE (Garbo's first talkie, 74 minutes in English) Directed by Clarence Brown. Produced by Metro-Goldwyn-Mayer. Screenplay by Frances Marion. Adapted from the play by Eugene O'Neill. Photographed by William Daniels. Edited by Hugh Wynn. New York Premiere: Capitol Theatre, March 4, 1930.

Anna Christie	Greta Garbo
Matt Burke	Charles Bickford
Marthy	Marie Dressler
Johnny the Priest	James T. Mack
Larry	Lee Phelps

ANNA CHRISTIE (German version, 82 minutes) directed by Jacques Feyder.

Anna Christie	Greta Garbo
Matt Burke	Hans Junkerman
Marthy	Salka Viertel
Chris	Theo Shall

STORY: Anna Christie, left as a child with selfish relatives, runs away and eventually becomes a prostitute. She seeks out her father and finds him on his fishing barge. Also on hand is his former mistress, an old waterfront character. Bitter and disillusioned, Anna meets a young seaman who falls in love with her. She returns his love, but is driven to tell him of her father's neglect and of her sordid past. His first reaction is to leave her, but later he returns, unable to stop loving her, and asks her to marry him.

CRITICS: "The voice that shook the world! It's Greta Garbo's, of course, and for the life of me I can't decide whether it's baritone or bass. She makes it heard for the first time on the screen in *Anna Christie*, and there isn't another like it. Disturbing, incongruous, its individuality is so pronounced that it would belong to no one less strongly individual than Garbo herself. Yet it doesn't wholly belong to her, but seems a trick of the microphone in exaggerating what in real life probably is merely a low-keyed voice, slightly husky."—*Picture Play* (1930)

12. ROMANCE (76 minutes) Directed by Clarence

Brown. Produced by Metro-Goldwyn-Mayer. Screenplay by Bess Meredyth and Edwin Justus Mayer. Adapted from Edward Sheldon's play, *Signora Cavallini*. Photographed by William Daniels. Edited by Hugh Wynn and Leslie F. Wilder. New York Premiere: Capitol Theatre, August 22, 1930.

Rita Cavallini	Greta Garbo
Cornelius Van Tuyl	Lewis Stone
Tom Armstrong	Gavin Gordon
Harry	Elliott Nugent
Susan Van Tuyl	Florence Lake
Miss Armstrong	Clara Blandick
Beppo	Henry Armetta

STORY: When Bishop Armstrong learns that his grandson, Elliott, wants to marry an actress, he tries to dissuade him by telling of his own life. He himself, he says, when he was still a rector, fell in love with an opera singer named Rita Cavallini. She loved him in return but admitted that she had been the mistress of the wealthy Cornelius Van Tuyl. When he asked her to return to him, she refused his offer. Armstrong, infuriated that she had seen Van Tuyl again, nonetheless asked her to spend the night with him. She pleaded with him not to treat her as others had, and began to pray. He thereupon saw his duty, and left. This recital by the Bishop does not alter the grandson's attitude: he still wants to marry an actress.

CRITICS: "One can scarcely credit the fact that an opera singer possessed so strained and muscular a tone in normal conversation. . . . Mme. Cavallini was clearly a creature of fiery impulses, unaccountable transitions of mood and behaviour. Miss Garbo offers us a glimpse, but not the whole, of this creation, and the infinite grace of her movements scarcely compensates for the lack of that inward passion which should flame across the character and make it comprehensible."—*Daily Telegraph* (1930)

13. INSPIRATION (74 minutes) Directed by Clarence Brown. Produced by Metro-Goldwyn-Mayer. Original screenplay by Gene Markey. Photographed by William Daniels. Edited by Conrad A. Nervig. New York Premiere: Capitol Theatre, February 6, 1931.

Yvonne	Greta Garbo
Andre	Robert Montgomery
Delval	Lewis Stone
Lulu	Marjorie Rambeau
Odette	Judith Vosselli
Marthe	Beryl Mercer
Coutant	John Miljan
Julian Montell	Edwin Maxwell

STORY: Yvonne, an artist's model, falls in love with Andre, a young diplomat. When he finds out that she has numerous previous lovers, he leaves her. He sees her later, impoverished and alone, and provides for her—telling her, however, that he is about to marry another. She pleads with him. In the paper he reads of a friend who committed suicide when her lover abandoned her. He determines to sacrifice his career and devote himself to Yvonne. When he goes to tell her, he finds one of her former lovers begging her to return to him. Andre insists that nothing matters except their love, but when he falls asleep Yvonne makes her own sacrifice. She writes him a farewell note and steals away.

CRITICS: "Garbo should be dewed with tears of regret. She makes her heroine sensitive, intelligent, alluring, with a shimmer of laughter like sunshine after an April shower. So superior indeed is Yvonne to the trite circumstances of her story that you feel the player, aware of the disparity, is spurred to greater effort."—*Picture Play* (1931)

14. SUSAN LENOX: HER FALL AND RISE (75 minutes) Directed by Robert Z. Leonard. Produced by Metro-Goldwyn-Mayer. Screenplay by Wanda Turchock. Adapted from the novel by David Graham Phillips. Dialogue by Zelda Sears and Leon Gordon. Photographed by William Daniels. Edited by Margaret Booth. New York Premiere: Capitol Theatre, October 16, 1931.

Susan Lenox	Greta Garbo
Rodney	Clark Gable
Ohlin	Jean Hersholt
Burlingham	John Miljan
Mondstrum	Alan Hale
Mike Kelly	Hale Hamilton
Astrid	Hilda Vaughn
Doctor	Russell Simpson
Madame Panoramia	Cecil Cunningham
Robert Lane	Ian Keith

STORY: Helga, a young farm girl, flees when her father tries to marry her off to a coarse man she detests. She meets an engineer, Rodney Spencer, who promises to help her. They live together and fall in love. While he is away on business, she learns that her father is coming after her: she escapes by boarding a passing carnival train. In order to stay with the troupe, she has an affair with the owner. Rodney finds her but cannot forgive her for having left. She becomes the mistress of a wealthy man, changes her name, and continues to search for Rodney, finally tracking him down in South America. He is broken in spirit and resentful, but Helga/Susan is finally able to convince him that she will be true to him. They reconcile and begin a new life together.

CRITICS: "The film is good for its purpose because neither hero nor heroine at any moment behaves like a sentient human being, because any straight answer to any straight question would have brought the film to an end at any moment. As far as Miss G. is concerned it is not so good, since when La Garbo is not queening it she is miserably out of place. . . . As a trull in homespun she is very nearly a fright."—James Agate (1931)

15. MATA HARI (90 minutes) Directed by George Fitzmaurice. Produced by Metro-Goldwyn-Mayer. Original screenplay by Benjamin Glazer and Leo Birinski. Dialogue by Doris Anderson and Gilbert Emery. Photographed by William Daniels. Edited by Frank Sullivan. New York Premiere: Capitol Theatre, December 31, 1931.

Mata Hari	Greta Garbo
Lieutenant Alexis Rosanoff	Ramon Novarro
General Shubin	Lionel Barrymore
Adriani	Lewis Stone
Dubois	C. Henry Gordon
Carlotta	Karen Morley
Caros	Alec B. Francis
Sister Angelica	Blanche Frederici

STORY: Mata Hari is a German spy posing as a dancer in Paris during World War I. Her assignment is to gain access to Russian messages about Allied military movements. She meets Russian Lt. Rosanoff and falls in love with him; when she discovers that it is he who has the desired documents, she steals them. Rosanoff's superior, General Shubin, is a former lover who has given her secret information in exchange for her favors. When he learns of the affair with Rosanoff, he threatens to turn them both in and Mata Hari shoots him. Rosanoff goes back to Russia, is shot down and blinded, then taken to a hospital. When Mata Hari comes to tell him she still loves him, she is arrested. Rosanoff comes to testify. Rather than let him know of her past, Mata Hari pleads guilty. They have a brief reunion in her cell before she is taken before a firing squad and executed.

CRITICS: "*Mata Hari*, intended as a high-pressure thriller, yet more than foggy in its scenario, was a concoction which would scarcely have given any actress much of a chance to write a human document. But you merely walked through it, like some superior and unperturbed mannequin." —Mary Cass Canfield, "Letter to Garbo," *Theatre Arts Monthly* (1932).

16. GRAND HOTEL (105 minutes) Directed by Edmund Goulding. Produced by Metro-Goldwyn-Mayer. Screenplay by William A. Drake. Adapted from the play by Vicki Baum. Photographed by William Daniels. Edited by Blanche Sewell. New York Premiere: Astor Theatre, April 12, 1932.

Grusinskaya	Greta Garbo
Baron von Gaigern	John Barrymore
Flaemmchen	Joan Crawford
Preysing	Wallace Beery
Otto Kringelein	Lionel Barrymore
Dr. Otternschlag	Lewis Stone
Senf	Jean Hersholt
Meierheim	Robert McWade
Zinnowitz	Purnell B. Pratt
Pimenov	Ferdinand Gottschalk
Suzette	Rafaela Ottiano
Chauffeur	Morgan Wallace
Gerstenkorn	Tully Marshall

STORY: The Grand Hotel in Berlin provides the setting for the personal stories of several characters. There is a self-made tycoon, an ambitious typist, and an elderly clerk out to have a last fling. And there is Grusinskaya, a famous but lonely ballet dancer. A jewel thief—the Baron von Gaigern —breaks into her suite bent on robbery, but when he finds her near suicide he changes tactics, posing as an admirer. They fall in love. While engaged in another burglary, the Baron is killed by the tycoon. Grusinskaya, unaware of his death, leaves the hotel making plans for her new life with him.

CRITICS: "From her first line, 'I have never been so tired in my life,' Greta Garbo sets the movie in vibration with her extraordinary presence. She is a premiere danseuse whose career is fading, a weary, disillusioned woman briefly reconciled to life by a passion for a shady nobleman—John Barrymore. Garbo was only twenty-six when she played this role (Barrymore was fifty), but the fatigue, the despair seemed genuine. Intellectually you have to reject *Grand Hotel* as an elaborate chunk of artifice and hocus-pocus, and anyone who comes to see this movie expecting an intelligent script or even 'good acting' should have his head examined. But if you want to see what screen glamour used to be and what, originally, 'stars' were, this is perhaps the best example of all time."—Pauline Kael, *Kiss Kiss Bang Bang* (1967)

17. AS YOU DESIRE ME (71 minutes) Directed by George Fitzmaurice. Produced by Metro-Goldwyn-Mayer. Scenario and adaptation (from Luigi Pirandello's play) by Gene Markey. Photography by William Daniels. Edited by George Hively. New York Premiere: Capitol Theatre, June 2, 1932.

Maria (Zara)	Greta Garbo
Count Bruno Varelli	Melvyn Douglas
Carl Salter	Erich von Stroheim
Tony Boffie	Owen Moore
Madame Mantari	Hedda Hopper
Lena	Rafaela Ottiano
Baron	Warburton Gamble
Captain	Albert Conti

STORY: Zara, a cabaret artist in Budapest, has amnesia and is also under the hypnotic influence of novelist Carl Salter. Painter Tony Boffie sees her and is convinced she is the long-missing wife of Count Bruno Varelli. Varelli comes to visit and accepts her as his wife. Salter, unwilling to let her go, brings his mistress to testify to another identity for Zara. He does not succeed. Zara stays with Varelli, but the questions linger—is she deluding herself? Who in reality is she?

CRITICS: "I am inclined to think that there is altogether too much discussion of Garbo these days. It is enough to say that this is not one of her most ambitious offerings, yet by no means one of her most trivial. As you have heard, this may be her last picture. She is said to be going back to that farm of hers. Well, I shall wait and see, and occupy my mind, if possible, with other matters in the meanwhile, and try to endure the suspense."—John Mosher, *The New Yorker* (1932)

18. QUEEN CHRISTINA (97 minutes) Directed by Rouben Mamoulian. Produced by Walter Wanger for Metro-Goldwyn-Mayer. Screenplay by Salka Viertel and H. M. Harwood. Adapted from an original screen story by Salka Viertel and Margaret F. Levine. Dialogue by S. N.

Behrman. Photographed by William Daniels. Edited by Blanche Sewell. Music composed by Herbert Stothart. New York Premiere: Astor Theatre, December 26, 1933.

Queen Christina	Greta Garbo
Don Antonio de la Prada	John Gilbert
Magnus	Ian Keith
Chancellor Oxenstierna	Lewis Stone
Ebba Sparre	Elizabeth Young
Aage	C. Aubrey Smith
Prince Charles	Reginald Owen
French Ambassador	Georges Renevent
Archbishop	David Torrence
General	Gustav Von Seyffertitz
Innkeeper	Ferdinant Munier
Christina (as a child)	Cora Sue Collins

STORY: Queen Christina of Sweden is unhappy at the prospect of marrying Prince Charles, a man she does not love. Learning that a new ambassador from Spain, Don Antonio, is due to arrive, she disguises herself in men's clothes and goes to an inn where he will stop. They share a room in the crowded inn; with embarrassment and then pleasure he discovers her true sex. They fall in love. After an idyll of several days, she wants to follow him to Spain. But on learning her identity, he informs her he has been sent to win her hand for his king. They now meet officially, but one of Christina's former lovers, Magnus, rouses the populace against Antonio. Christina abdicates. She arranges a rendezvous with Antonio, but arriving there she finds him dead, killed in a duel with Magnus. She boards the ship carrying his body to Spain, leaving her homeland behind forever.

CRITICS: "The magnificent Garbo, after an absence of over a year, makes a glorious reappearance on the screen. Garbo, enchanting as ever, is still enveloped by her unfathomable mystery."—*Photoplay* (1933)

19. THE PAINTED VEIL (83 minutes) Directed by Richard Boleslawski. Produced by Hunt Stromberg for Metro-Goldwyn-Mayer. Screenplay by John Meehan, Salka Viertel, and Edith Fitzgerald. Adapted from the novel by W. Somerset Maugham. Photographed by William Daniels. Edited by Hugh Wynn. New York Premiere: Capitol Theatre, December 7, 1934.

Katrin Fane	Greta Garbo
Walter Fane	Herbert Marshall
Jack Townsend	George Brent
General Yu	Warner Oland
Herr Koerber	Jean Hersholt
Frau Koerber	Beaulah Bondi
Mrs. Townsend	Katherine Alexander
Olga	Cecilia Parker
Amah	Soo Yong
Waddington	Forrester Harvey

STORY: Katrin Fane accompanies her doctor husband to China, where he neglects her for his work. She has an affair with a diplomatic attaché, which Fane soon discovers. As punishment, he forces her to go with him to fight a cholera epidemic. The attaché, fearful for his career, withdraws. Working together rekindles the love between Katrin and Fane. Townsend reappears, but all of Katrin's devotion is now to her husband.

CRITICS: "Watch her stalking about with long and nervous steps, her shoulders bent and her body awkward with grief, while she waits to be told if her husband will die from the coolie's dagger thrust. It is as if all this had never been done before. Watch the veiled terror in her face as she sits at dinner with her husband, not knowing if he is aware of her infidelity. . . . . She shrouds all this with dignity, making it precious and memorable."—Andre Sennwald, *The New York Times* (1934)

20. ANNA KARENINA (95 minutes) Directed by Clarence Brown, Produced by David O. Selznick for Metro-Goldwyn-Mayer. Screenplay by Clemence Dane and Salka Viertel. Adapted from the novel by Leo Tolstoy. Dialogue by S. N. Behrman. Photographed by William Daniels. Edited by Robert J. Kern. New York Premiere: Capitol Theatre, August 30, 1935.

Anna Karenina	Greta Garbo
Vronsky	Fredric March
Sergei	Freddie Bartholomew
Kitty	Maureen O'Sullivan
Countess Vronsky	May Robson
Karenin	Basil Rathbone
Stiva	Reginald Owen
Yashvin	Reginald Denny

STORY: The talkie version of Tolstoy's famous novel, which Garbo had made in silent days as *Love*.

CRITICS: "Miss Garbo has never looked lovelier or played more beautifully than she does in the new and handsome screen version of Tolstoy's celebrated *Anna Karenina*. But I would be unfair to you if I did not confess that my verdict on the picture is based in great part on prejudice. Everything I say in connection with the work is predicated on the fact that it gives Miss Garbo the best opportunity she has had in several seasons and, since she is completely fascinating in *Anna Karenina*, it seems to me a splendid motion picture."—Richard Watts, Jr., *The New York Herald Tribune* (1935)

21. CAMILLE (109 minutes) Directed by George Cukor. Produced by Irving Thalberg for Metro-Goldwyn-Mayer. Screenplay by Zoë Atkins, Frances Marion and James Hilton. Adapted from the novel and play, *La Dame aux Camélias*, by Alexandre Dumas. Photographed by William Daniels. Edited by Margaret Booth. New York Premiere: Capitol Theatre, January 22, 1937.

Marguerite	Greta Garbo
Armand	Robert Taylor
Monsieur Duval	Lionel Barrymore
Nichette	Elizabeth Allan
Nanine	Jessie Ralph
Baron de Varville	Henry Daniell
Olympe	Lenore Ulric
Prudence	Laura Hope Crews
Gaston	Rex O'Malley
Gustave	Russell Hardie
Saint Gaudens	E. E. Clive
Henri	Douglas Walton
Corinne	Marion Ballou
Marie Jeanette	Joan Brodel
Louise	June Wilkins
Valentin	Fritz Lieber, Jr.
Madamoiselle Duval	Elsie Esmonds

STORY: The well-known Dumas tale of Camille, the fashionable Parisian courtesan, and her sacrificing love for young Armand Duval. Their chance for happiness is blighted first by an old lover, the Baron de Varville, and then by Armand's father, who tells Camille she will ruin the boy's career and life by marrying him. Camille complies with the

Baron's wishes. She tells Armand she prefers the rich, gay life of Paris to his company. She contracts tuberculosis, and becomes sadly impoverished. Armand finds her, promising to stay with her always. She dies, finding solace in his love.

CRITICS: "The incomparable Greta Garbo has returned to the screen in a breathtakingly beautiful and superbly modulated portrayal of Camille. As the tragic Dumas heroine, she floods a romantic museum piece with glamour and artistry, making it a haunting and moving photoplay by the sheer magic of her acting. It was not my good fortune to witness the great Eleanora Duse in the play, but I have seen many other illustrious actresses in French and English versions, and none have remotely matched Miss Garbo . . ."— Howard Barnes, *The New York Herald Tribune* (1937)

22. CONQUEST (115 minutes) Directed by Clarence Brown. Produced by Bernard H. Hyman for Metro-Goldwyn-Mayer. Screenplay by Samuel Hoffenstein, Salka Viertel, and S. N. Behrman. Adapted from the novel *Pani Walewska* by Waclaw Gasiorowski and dramatization by Helen Jerome. Photographed by Karl Freund. Edited by Tom Held. New York Premiere: Capitol Theatre, November 4, 1937.

Marie Walewska	Greta Garbo
Napoleon	Charles Boyer
Talleyrand	Reginald Owen
Captain d'Ornano	Alan Marshal
Count Walewska	Henry Stephenson
Paul Lachinski	Leif Erickson
Laetitia Bonaparte	Dame May Whitty
Prince Poniatowski	C. Henry Gordon
Countess Pelagia	Maria Ouspenskaya

STORY: At a state ball in Poland, Napoleon meets the beautiful Marie Waleska. Polish patriots encourage her to visit him to plead for their country's independence. They have an affair, which leads Count Waleska to divorce her. Marie becomes Napoleon's mistress and has a son by him, but his drive for power leads him to abandon her for the Hapsburgh princess Marie Louise. After his defeat at Waterloo, Marie visits him and brings their son with her. She and Napoleon bid each other farewell on the eve of his departure for St. Helena.

CRITICS: "Madame Garbo's elegant anemia, I fear, can pall a little. Her performance seems static, though the story covers a period of years. Beautiful, fragile, and tired, she stands in the first scene among the Cossacks invading her husband's house and quite unchanged, fragile and tired still, she waves her last farewell to Napoleon, as though she would assert that loyalty is but a symptom of exhaustion. I think that for the first time Madame Garbo has a leading man who contributes more to the interest and vitality of the film than she does. She is, we may assume, grateful for such assistance."—John Mosher, *The New Yorker* (1937)

23. NINOTCHKA (110 minutes) Directed by Ernst Lubitsch. Produced by Ernst Lubitsch for Metro-Goldwyn-Mayer. Screenplay by Charles Brackett, Billy Wilder, and Water Reisch. Adapted from the story by Melchior Lengyel. Photographed by William Daniels. Edited by Gene Ruggiero. New York Premiere: Radio City Music Hall, November 9, 1939.

Ninotchka	Greta Garbo
Count Leon d'Algout	Melvyn Douglas
Grand Duchess Swana	Ina Claire

Commissar Razinin	Bela Lugosi
Iranoff	Sig Rumann
Buljanoff	Felix Bressart
Kopalski	Alexander Granach
Count Rakonin	Gregory Gaye
Hotel Manager	Rolfe Sedan
Mercier	Edwin Maxwell
Gaston	Richard Carle

STORY: Three Soviet envoys are sent to Paris to sell some jewelry in order to buy farm machinery. When they start neglecting their duties to live the gay life of Paris, a stern female comrade, Ninotchka, is sent after them. She chastises them, but when she meets the debonair Leon, he gradually thaws her cold, formal manner. The three comrades and Ninotchka eventually decide to abandon ideological principles and open a restaurant in Constantinople. Ninotchka and Leon will marry.

CRITICS: "Now that she has done it, it seems incredible that Greta Garbo never appeared in a comedy before *Ninotchka*. For in this gay burlesque of Bolsheviks abroad, the great actress reveals a command of comic inflection which fully matches the emotional depth or tragic power of her earlier triumphs. It is a joyous, subtly shaded and utterly enchanting portrayal which she creates, to illuminate a rather slight satire and make it the year's most capitvating screen comedy."—Howard Barnes, *New York Herald Tribune* (1939)

24. TWO-FACED WOMAN (94 minutes) Directed by George Cukor. Produced by Gottfried Reinhardt for Metro-Goldwyn-Mayer. Screenplay by S. N. Behrman, Salka Viertel, and George Oppenheimer. Adapted from a play by Ludwig Fulda. Photographed by Joseph Rutten-

berg. Edited by George Boemler. New York Premiere: Capitol Theatre, December 31, 1941.

Karin	Greta Garbo
Larry Blake	Melvyn Douglas
Griselda Vaughn	Constance Bennett
O. O. Miller	Roland Young
Dick Williams	Robert Sterling
Miss Ellis	Ruth Gordon
Miss Dunbar	Frances Carson
Dancer	Bob Alton

STORY: Publisher Larry Blake goes to a ski resort and winds up marrying Karin, a ski instructress. Once back in New York, he is drawn to an old flame, the sophisticated Griselda Vaughn. Karin plots to win back her husband: she passes as her own twin, a woman as worldly and sophisticated as Griselda. After various complications, she achieves her goal, and Larry returns to her.

CRITICS: "It is almost as shocking as seeing your mother drunk."—*Time* (1942)

Bibliography

A. Books

References to Garbo appear in countless memoirs and other accounts of Hollywood in the twenties and thirties. The following list is confined to biographies of Garbo, books which make substantial reference to her, or works referred to in the text.

Acosta, Mercedes de: *Here Lies the Heart*, Reynal & Co., 1960

Bainbridge, John: *Garbo*, Doubleday & Co., 1955

Beaton, Cecil: *Photography*, Doubleday & Co., 1951
——— *Persona Grata*, G. P. Putnam's Sons, 1954

Billquist, Fritiof: *Garbo*, G. P. Putnam's Sons, 1960

Bankhead, Tallulah: *Tallulah*, Harper's, 1952

Crowther, Bosley: *Hollywood Rajah*, Holt, Rinehart, and Winston, 1960

Day, Beth: *This Was Hollywood*, Sidgwick and Jackson, London 1960

Dragonette, Jessica: *Faith Is a Song*, David McKay Co., 1951

Durgnat, Raymond and Kobal, John: *Greta Garbo*, Dutton Vista Pictureback, 1965

188

Goodman, Ezra: *The Fifty-Year Decline and Fall of Hollywood*, Simon & Schuster, 1961

Griffith, Richard and Mayer, Arthur, *The Movies*, Bonanza Books, 1957

Hauser, Gayelord: *Look Younger: Live Longer*, Farrar, Strauss, 1950

Hopper, Hedda: *From Under My Hat*, Doubleday & Co., 1953

Kael, Pauline: *Kiss Kiss Bang Bang*, Little, Brown & Co., 1968

Maxwell, Elsa, *RSVP*, Little, Brown & Co., 1954

Palmborg, Rilla Page: *The Private Life of Greta Garbo*, Doubleday, Doran, 1931

Stephens, William Eben, *Hollywood Legends*, Marvin Miller, Inc., Covina, Cal.

Tyler, Parker: introduction to *The Films of Greta Garbo*, Citadel

Vidor, King: *A Tree is a Tree*, Longmans, Green and Co., 1954

Walker, Alexander: *The Celluloid Sacrifice*, Michael Joseph, 1967

B. Magazine Articles

During the twenties and the thirties, *Photoplay*, *Motion Picture*, *Classic* and other fan magazines carried articles about Garbo in virtually every other issue. The following list includes only those of a substantial biographical nature, or articles referred to in the text.

Colliers: "This is Garbo," by Nathaniel Benchley, March 1, 1952

Films and Filming: "How Good Was She?" by Richard Whitehall, September 1963

Films in Review: "*The Career of Greta Garbo,*" by Theodore Huff, December 1951

Newsweek: "Garbo," by Hubert Saal, July 22, 1968

New York Museum of Art Film Notes: series 4, April 1965, by Iris Barry

———— Notes for Garbo Festival, 1968

New York Times Magazine: "The Saga of Greta Lovisa Gustafsson," by Hollis Alpert, September 5, 1965

New Yorker: a short profile of Garbo by Virgilia Peterson Ross, March 7, 1931

Photoplay: "Exploding the Garbo Myth," by Katherine Albert, April 1931

———— "What Garbo Thinks of Hollywood," by Katherine Albert, August 1931

"The Story of Greta Garbo," as told to Ruth Biery, April 1927 and following

"Garbomaniacs," by Leonard Hall, January 1930

"See Garbo First," by Leonard Hall, July 1931

"That Gustafsson Girl," by Ake Sundborg, April 1930 and following

Player's Showcase: "Garbo," by Syd Barker, summer 1965

Show: "Garbo Walks," by Alan Levy, June 1963

Sight and Sound: Kenneth Tynan on Garbo, April-June 1954

Vanity Fair: "The Great Garbo," by Clare Booth Brokaw, February 1932

———— "Then Came Garbo," November 1932

Index

191

Paramount Pictures, 11, 49, 93, 127
Parker, Dorothy, 61
Parsons, Louella, 145
Paul U. Bergstrom's Department Store (PUB), 26, 27
Petschler, Erik A., 27
Photoplay, 18-19
Pickford, Mary, 13
Pirandello, Luigi, 72
Pitts, Zazu, 48
Polansky, Joseph, 42-43
Pommer, Erich, 49
Porter, Allen, 134, 135, 141, 155
Porter, Cole, 142
Pringle, Aileen, 60

Queen Christina (1933), 67-68, 73, 84, 111, 112, 113, 117, 118, 121, 123, 124, 128
cast, story and criticism of, 179-81
Quirk, James, 18

Rasunda Film City, 32
Rathbone, Basil, 102
Rathbone, Ouida, 102
Redemption, 66
Reid, Wallace, 12
Reinhardt, Gottfried, 98
Reinhart, Max, 107, 130
Reisch, Walter, on Garbo, 97-100
Ring, Captain Ragnar, 26-27
Romance (1930), 72, 76, 85, 119, cast, story and criticism of, 172-174
Ross, Harold, 109
Ross, Virgilia Peterson, 18
Rothschild, Cecile de, 136, 137
relationship of Garbo and, 149
Rothschild, Robert de, 149
Rothschild family, 146
Royal Dramatic Theatre (Stockholm), 25, 28

Saga of Gösta Berling, The (1924), 30-37
cast, story and criticism of, 160-61
St. Johns, Adela Rogers, 60, 62, 68, 73, 126-27
Sale, Mary, 78, 104
Sand, Georges, 128
Schenck, Nicholas, 41
Scheuer, Phil, 76
on Garbo Film Festival, 22

Schlee, George, 136, 137-38, 140
background of, 138
relationship between Garbo and, 138-39
Schlee, Valentina, 138, 139, 140
relationship between Garbo and, 138-40
Screen Gems, 150
Seastrom, Victor, 39, 40, 45, 50, 72
Seeber, Guido, 39
Seligman, Eustace, 134
Selznick, David O., 127
Sennett, Mack, 27, 29
Shearer, Douglas, 71
Shearer, Norma, 43, 62, 71, 95
Sheen, Bishop Fulton, 150
Sheldon, Edward, 73
Sherwood Robert E., 49
on Garbo, 122
Simmons, Jim, 114
Single Standard, The (1929), 100
cast, story and criticism of, 169
Sir Arne's Treasure, Stiller as director of, 29
Sitwell, Edith, 152
Sitwell, Osbert, 152
Sitwell, Sacheverell, 152
Smith, Alexis, 43
Smith, Alice (pseudonym for Garbo), 105
Smith, Arthur Gordon, 150
Smith, Pete, 43, 44
Snow, C. P., 156
Spiegel, Sam, 146
Stearns, Johnny, 77
on Garbo, 93-94
Stiller, Mauritz, 23, 25, 47, 53, 58, 88, 89, 96, 107, 138
on acting, 29
background of, 28-29
Broadway and, 50
death of, 50
as director of *The Tempest*, 48-49
Garbo on, 50
and Gilbert, 63
Gilbert on, 52
in Hollywood, 42, 44, 45-46
as innovator, 29
Mayer and, 40, 44, 46
meeting of Garbo and, 25, 30-32
Metro-Goldwyn-Mayer and, 40-41, 44
in New York, 41-42